In Due Season

Prayer for Spring, Lent, Easter and Summer Feastdays

Ken Phillips

DEDICATED WITH GRATITUDE
TO THE MEMORY OF
FATHER JOHN KIEFER, OP,
WHO WITH POETRY, POTTERY,
AND AN EXPANSIVE SENSE OF PRIESTHOOD
EXPANDED MY WORLD OF PRAYER.

TWENTY-THIRD PUBLICATIONS
1 Montauk Avenue, Suite 200, New London, CT 06320
(860) 437-3012 » (800) 321-0411 » www.23rdpublications.com

© Copyright 2015 Ken Phillips. All rights reserved.
The purchaser of this book may make copies of prayer services for assembly use within their community. Except for this use, no part of this publication may be reproduced in any manner without prior written permission of the publisher. Write to the Permissions Editor.

ISBN: 978-1-62785-059-9
Library of Congress Catalog Card Number: 2014940878
Printed in the U.S.A.

CONTENTS

Foreword
PAGE v

Part I
The Spring Transformation
PAGE 1

Part II
Welcome Holy Springtide
PAGE 37

Part III
The Long Arc of the Spirit: Summer Feasts
PAGE 83

Part IV
As Summer Closes
PAGE 109

Foreword

Although they are perhaps a vanishing breed, I have always been attracted to wall calendars. In a multiplicity of styles, formats, and themes, their images have assisted in the business of passage through a year. Whether holding reproductions of art treasures, photographs of faraway places, or even silly humorous cartoons, the pages parked by pushpin to various walls of my life have helped me at various times to know just where I am as the months fly past. If I become lost in the mire of meetings, obligations, transitions, and travels, an examination of the beautiful wall calendar can land me, at least for a moment; I can get my temporal bearings in a glance.

Calendars of seasons, festivals, feasts, holidays, liturgies, and so forth have a similar anchoring function. Liturgical calendars especially help me, particularly because they mark the entire year with importance, history, legacy, identity, and soul. Most significantly, there is ritual available for virtually every turn. Like a good image, ritual helps place me more concretely into the moment, and, at certain moments, it can lift me beyond time.

Many of us live multiple calendars at once: annual, academic, work, hunting, social, personal, body, cultural, or religious. This collection of rhythms can be mind-boggling, but it can also remind us of how our biological realities are amplified or challenged by other systems. We don't just accumulate days; we connect ourselves with lives and histories outside our own, and these various calendars remind us that we are not just the ticked-off passage of sunrise to sunsets. Our cyclic travelling through time connects us to spiritual and cosmic realities. Our rites and poetry remind us of this.

In Due Season, Volume II continues the marking of natural seasons, agricultural calendars, and liturgical feasts, festivals, and flavorings of the Christian year. With more poetic meditations, prayer and Scripture services, litanies, and table services, we continue to plumb metaphoric and liturgical ground that is always reflected in the seasons of human life and the life of the soul.

Volume II continues to encourage prayer leadership by lay people, and many of the pieces are apt for domestic gatherings, retreats, and church groups, as well as personal meditation. The language continues to be ritual language. It is poetic, inviting us to consider the holy through the stuff of everyday life as well as through the images of our faith stories. It invites us to step outside of our "schedules." These pieces are not laundry lists of items to be hurried through with great expedience. They are opportunities to literally "take time" and bathe in the richness of our earthbound, spiritual, and personal journeys.

Beginning with Ash Wednesday services, this volume continues the marking of the year through Lent/springtime, into Holy Week/Eastertide, to Pentecost/summer, and lands us again in late summer/early fall. It is presented with the hope that we might further expand our understandings of the richness of "marked time," the power of ritual and symbols, and the joy of language that is spoken carefully and prayed thoughtfully.

Part I

THE SPRING TRANSFORMATION

Near Ash Wednesday

A Service of Ashes & Stones for the Restoration of the World's Wounded

APPLICATION

Ash Wednesday, Lenten reconciliation service, service of prayer for the world, etc. The litany can be used on its own or folded into a larger service. It can be linked with appropriate readings from Scripture or other sources (including media headlines).

SET UP

This is prayed by a group gathered in a circle around a low table covered in purple or battered burlap where there is a larger, empty vessel for ashes and various smaller vessels filled with ashes around it. (Small Asian bowls, glass food prep bowls, or ceramic vessels all work well.) These smaller vessels may be given to participants before the start. There is a resonant gong, chime, or chiming bowl to sound at each petition. There are also stones in a basket for distribution in the second half of the prayer.

CALL TO PRAYER

Depending on the circumstances, the service begins with an indication of the nature of Ash Wednesday/Lent, a call to change, or the practice of listening to the world to pray for its many needs. There is some sort of call to mindfulness (quiet, intentional breathing or meditational music or song). A designated leader lights a candle and begins the prayer when all are ready. All read the parts in bold.

CALL TO PRAYER

Leader: Let us pray:
(silence)

God of Mystery, Holy One, source of mercy and compassion: we lift our hearts in prayer today in the face of realities in our world that are difficult to understand, painful to encompass, and often impossible to explain.

We remember our brothers and sisters around the globe who, in this very hour, suffer from the acts of humans, conditions of the Earth in crisis, or movements of nature.

We turn our hearts and spirits to You on behalf of people who experience the painful loss of loved ones, homes, and livelihood.

Hear us as we pray.

A LITANY OF GATHERED ASHES

(From the small bowls, ashes are poured into the larger vessel at each petition.)

1) **Receive these ashes of loss, Most High.**

    For loving and gifted people whose lives are suddenly and

painfully ended by missiles, bomb blasts, and bullets.

Hear the cry of Earth's wounded ones.

(A chime is sounded, and we keep silence as its vibrations diminish.)

2) **Receive these ashes of suffering, O God.**

For lives scarred by the upheaval of Earth, violent storms, and fires of destruction seared into memory.

Hear the cry of Earth's dismayed and displaced ones.

(A chime is sounded, and we keep silence as its vibrations diminish.)

3) **Receive these ashes of grief, Loving One.**

For those who wander in the brittle remnants of homes bombed, flooded, burnt, toppled, collecting fragments of their lives, their legacies.

Hear the cry of Earth's dispossessed ones.

(A chime is sounded, and we keep silence as its vibrations diminish.)

4) **Receive these ashes of anxiety and sorrow, God of Mercy.**

For those slain by human knowledge gone astray: for those dead because of poison gasses, hidden explosives, drone bombers; for all deaths in warfare that are accounted for, and for those lost that go unnamed.

Hear the cry of Earth's slain.

(A chime is sounded, and we keep silence as its vibrations diminish.)

5) **Receive these ashes of bitterness and wrath, God of Justice.**

For those who are left with only disbelief, anger, and thoughts of revenge after acts of violence on our streets, in our homes, in our courts and prisons.

Hear the cry of Earth's bruised and offended ones.

(A chime is sounded, and we keep silence as its vibrations diminish.)

6) **Receive these ashes of mourning, God of Compassion.**

For people who endure loss after loss, haunted always by the sharp pains of absence; for those who despair of Your presence, Your consolation, and human care.

Hear the cry of Earth's hopeless ones.

(A chime is sounded, and we keep silence as its vibrations diminish.)

7) **Receive these ashes of disbelief and hopelessness, Creating God.**

For the young ones who grow up twisted with the impact of street violence and crime; for those shaped by the inadequacies of prisons and legal systems; for those scarred by malpractice in religion, medicine, and law; for those schooled too well in poverty in the midst of plenty.

Hear the cry of Earth's poor.

(A chime is sounded, and we keep silence as its vibrations diminish.)

8) Option for other petitions…

(At the close of the petitions, the larger vessel of gathered ashes is lifted up as the following is prayed:)

LEADER:
We have gathered these ashes blown from many winds, across many lands and peoples, and we pray:

The Spring Transformation

O Transforming One,
  hear our plea:
that through their pain
  and by Your power,

These ashes will make fertile the soil of Earth's future;

that by our action
  and through Your mercy,

We will make choices to aid the people who are awash in need;

that by their will
  and in Your Grace,

Earth's wounded will have the strength to endure and thrive,

and that by Your Spirit,

Our compassion and knowledge will be transformed into deeds.

OPTION FOR SIGNING WITH ASHES

(Some words may be shared about transformation, the graces and disciplines of Lenten practice, the desire to embrace Lenten activities that go beyond giving up simple things to engaging in service that may make a real difference to others. There may also be sharing about the sign value of ashes—as symbols of transformation and repentance, their ancient symbolism, etc.)

(Ashes are signed [forehead, palms, heart…] with appropriate saying and response. Music may be played.)

A LITANY OF GATHERED STONES

(In the center space there is a basket/vessel of small stones of various types. The basket is passed as the following petitions are read, and a stone is removed by each person; or the basket remains in place and people may go to the basket when they are so moved and retrieve a stone in that manner.)

(The leader or another person present may share some words about our habits of carrying stones around with us: hard habits, words, thoughts, memories, etc. In Lent's journey of transformation, we may acknowledge these personal hardnesses of heart, mind, and practices and open them up for change. In the litany below, we acknowledge that such things are also part of the behavior of the human family—and in praying we open these things up to God's grace as well.)

LEADER: The human heart can be hard territory, Most High. Our words have sharpened edges. Our individual and corporate sight can be obscured with the grit of greed, with arrogance and harsh judgments. Our decisions can be weighted down with vengeance, carelessness, and ignorance. We acknowledge that we hold tightly to the stones of sinful behavior when we are invited to open our hands to Your grace.

We pray that you lead us to conversion (this Lent),
O Merciful One:

1) When we pursue violence rather than understanding,

   Help us to let go of the stones of anger and rage.

2) When we choose religious and nationalistic prejudice rather than compassion,

   Help us to let go of the stones of hardened hearts.

3) When we would strike out in physical or emotional violence rather than do the work of healing,

   Help us to let go of the stones of fear.

4) When we prefer to live as enemies rather than work together for the well-being of the human family,

Help us to let go of the stones of aggression.

5) When we opt to give in to cynicism and despair rather than embrace the truth of our goodness,

Help us to let go of the stones of self-contempt.

6) When we might allow the work of justice and peacemaking to be done by others rather than to engage in it ourselves,

Help us to let go of the stones of inertia.

7) When we turn away our sight from the needs of those in our midst rather than respond as we are able,

Help us to let go of the stones of blindness.

8) Option for other petitions…

LEADER: Let us pray together:

O Tender God, in the journey that is before us, we carry these stones as reminders of our tendency to cling to the things that weigh our spirits down. Grant that we be open to the wisdom, insight, and grace that we need to let go enough to be more truly Your people. May Your voice soften the territory within us that remains closed and tight against life lived to the full. AMEN.

(Inspired by a 9/11 Prayer by Rev. Patricia Pierce, pastor of Tabernacle Church, Philadelphia.)

DISMISSAL

LEADER Let us go forth now, resolved to become waiting earth, receptive to the seed of the Good News, open to the rains of compassion and tender mercy from within and from on high.

Thanks Be To God!

(Sing a closing song or exchange a sign of peace.)

■ ■ ■

LENTEN PRAYERS OF THE PEOPLE

In Temptation

APPLICATION

The Lenten Sunday cycle of readings frequently begins with the account of Jesus in the desert following his baptism, where he is tempted in crucial ways. It is the archetype of our Lenten journey and of much of our time on Earth. We are presented with opportunities and situations that are not always life-giving or in our spirit's best interest. We are often tempted in those areas of our lives where we are the most vulnerable.

The litany of prayer below can be used on its own at a gathering in Lent, in conjunction with the gospel of the temptation in the desert, as part of a larger Lenten service, or even as a teaching on temptation.

An intermittent sung refrain (e.g., Bob Hurd's "O God Hear Us" or the Taizé chant "O Lord Hear My Prayer") may be used in the course of the litany of prayers. The petitions may also be rendered in an antiphonal fashion (side A, side B).

The assembly reads parts in bold type, so a printed text is needed for the assembly. This can be in a worship aid of some sort or rendered as PowerPoint slides with images or color.

READER:
Matthew 4:1–11

LEADER: My Friends, let us join our hearts and pray together for strength on our Lenten journey: God our Maker, hear our prayers as we begin [continue] our steps together in this Lenten wilderness. By the binding of our hearts and souls to You and to one another, may we know Your saving power.

PETITIONS

1) When tempted to arrogance or self-righteousness,

> **Let the Church remember the humility and service of the Christ who calls us.**

Aid us, O God,

> **And lead us to life.**

2) When tempted to misuse of power and corruption of law,

> **Let nations and powers remember how fragile we are, how interconnected, and how all things fade.**

Aid us, O God,

> **And lead us to life.**

3) When tempted with hopelessness in the face of challenges and calamities,

> **Let our own nation remember Your gifts to us and our possibilities together.**

Aid us, O God,

> **And lead us to life.**

4) When tempted to the false comfort of consumption and greed for material goods,
Let us remember simplicity in our living and the needs of the poor.

Aid us, O God,

> **And lead us to life.**

5) When tempted to anger and violence,
Grant us the grace of restraint and the power of Your peace.

Aid us, O God,

> **And lead us to life.**

6) When tempted by the distractions of busyness and noise in our daily lives,

> **Help us to embrace reflection and silence to find You.**

Aid us, O God,

> **And lead us to life.**

7) When illness and pain make us blind to Your real and abiding presence,

> **Open our eyes and stretch out Your hand.**

Aid us, O God,

> **And lead us to life.**

8) When frustrations, burdens, and barriers make us lose hope and trust in You,

> **Give us the memory of Your assistance in the past and the power to persevere in the present.**

Aid us, O God,

> **And lead us to life.**

9) When loneliness and isolation make us feel cut off from the human family,

> **Grant us the power to reach out to others who are also in need of aid, comfort, and companionship.**

Aid us, O God,

> **And lead us to life.**

10) When near to death, when suffering the loss of those we love, when fearful of our own mortality,

> **Grant us release from fear and help us trust that, because of Christ, death is not the final word.**

Aid us, O God,

> **And lead us to eternal life.**

LEADER: O God, we know well our fragility and weakness. We know how we lose our way and forget our true identity in You. Help us this Lent to be open in new ways to Your grace that strengthens, renews, and restores us. We pray together in Jesus' name:

AMEN.

■ ■ ■

The Spring Transformation

AT THE FEAST OF THE ANNUNCIATION

An Invocation to Mary: Maiden, Mother, Crone

APPLICATION

An individual or group prayer on or around the feast of the Annunciation (March 25). A simple prayer, it can be expanded in various ways. The prayer can be interwoven with music or song that matches each phase. On certain occasions, the poem could be danced by women of various ages. Different icons/art images of Mary can be engaged (see below). The prayer can be used in other contexts as well and may be a portion of a larger Marian or Mother's Day devotion.

SET UP

If prayed privately, a lit candle may assist the meditation, especially if prayed before dawn or at evening. An icon of Mary may prove helpful as a focus. In a group setting, a gathering of images (or something like a PowerPoint slide presentation) can accompany the meditation (e.g., Mary depicted in various stages of her life: young girl with St. Anne, maiden of the Annunciation, birth of Jesus, Mary at the cross, etc.). If resources allow, the placement of Marian images can help to create a kind of "Stations of the Life Of Mary."

CALL TO PRAYER

If used within a service, a simple explanation might be given about the Mother of Jesus, the meaning and story of the Annunciation, and the cardinal archetypes of a woman's life. Prayer could begin with a call to mindfulness (quiet, intentional breathing or appropriate Marian music).

I. ICON OF CHILD MARY

Maiden of Mirth,
Spring Breath of
The Most High,
Wind-born Music of
Creation's First Dance,
Sister of Possibilities,
gentle, fair,
unfettered one—
we wait for you.

Come to us!
Be with us
and bless us here
with laughter and fellowship,
with delight in the Word
sprung in sweetness
where you pass.

Sister, spring-like and new,
be with us here!
Upturn the world
and make us supple
in our living!

II. ICON OF YOUNG MARY

Mother of Mercy,
Hard Breath of
the Power of Love,
Vessel of Life and Deepest Birth,
Milk of Heaven
    for Human Souls,
gracious, loving,
tender one—
we call to you.

DEDICATED WITH GRATITUDE TO EILEEN O'BRIEN

Cradle us!
Comfort us!
And bless us here
with companions and family,
with nourishing words
born from life's center,
where you are forever.

Holy Mother, summer-full
   and strong,
Be with us here!
Renew the world in the gift
   of your womb.
Make us ready to hold
   all the life
entrusted to us.

III. ICON OF MARY WITH CRUCIFIED JESUS

Lady of Wisdom,
Breath of the Holy,
Source of Mystery,
Footpath of the Human Journey,
Ancient Face of the Ever New,
Vessel of Grief,
Mother of Sorrow,
Lady Lifted Up On High,
guiding, teaching,
thoughtful one—
we call to you.

Sustain us!
Inspire us!
And bless us here
with your story unfolding,
   with eyes and ears
deep enough
and
generous enough
for our own story,
where you have dwelt.

Ancient one,
autumn-free and
winter-strong,
be with us here!
Strengthen the world,
and make us brave
to learn from sorrow,
to behold death,
to carry the burdens
that are entrusted
to us.

IV. ICON OF THE DORMITION OF MARY

Sleep, Lady,
gentle sleep.
For you who have carried
so much,
so long,
so quietly.

Sleep and remember:
strange dreams
and long journeys,

swaddling clothes
and hurried departures,
countless meals amidst
lengths of wood
and gazes of the curious.
Remember all:
the cares of many,
the thorns that crowned him,
the cloak that covered him,
the cross that bore him,
the crowd that reviled him,
the stone that held him,
the tears that honored him,
the olive branch,
the lily,
the shaft of grain,
the seed head scattered…

Oh, Lady,
holy, mysterious,
sleep now
and rise
to his voice
and
his welcome.
This,
no dream,
no rude waking.

Only, Lady,
dear and faithful,
   only bliss.

AMEN.

■ ■ ■

The Spring Transformation

A Springtime Prayer at Table

Blessed are You,
Lord God, maker of the
 universe.
Through Your goodness
the earth brings forth food
to nourish,
to sustain,
to delight.

We thank You for what we
share today with each other,
and we ask Your grace
to share what we have
with those who have need.
Thank You for all the ways You
 feed us.

Blessed are You,
Holy God, maker of
 humankind.
Through Your goodness
we are part of the human family.
We love,
we labor,
we grow together.

We thank You for who we are
with each other,
and we ask Your grace
to share our gifts and talents
with those who have need.
Thank You for all the ways You
 love us.

Make us mindful, ever-springing
 God,
of that which blooms before us,
emerges within us,
leans heavenward,
and roots freshward down
in this season of amazing
 newness.
And let us,
who are so often blinded by the
too-much and too-many,
be always young enough
to feast at this unrolling table
of Your constant remaking
with always
gratitude.

Amen.

■ ■ ■

Prayers of the People

For a Gathering in Lent

APPLICATION

Used on its own at a Lenten gathering or as part of a larger worship service.

If prayed on its own, the prayer could be expanded by the lighting of a candle, ringing of a chime, planting of a seed in a vessel of earth, or another symbolic action after each petition.

The assembly reads parts in bold type, so a printed text is needed for the assembly. This can be in a worship aid of some sort or rendered as PowerPoint slides with images.

Leader:
Sisters and brothers, let us pray:

(There is a pause for silence.)

God of the Covenant, we are among the people You have called in love, and we stand in need. Hear us as we raise our voices in heartfelt prayer, for ourselves and for our world.

1) Loving God, we pray for transformation and change in our selves and in the world.

(Pause for quiet prayer.)

Help us in this difficult age to trust in Your abiding presence.

> **Teach us to hold fast to Your word living deep within us. Give us the grace to remember that Your love prevails, even over death.**

Source of our faith,

> **Fulfill Your promise.**

2) God of Light, we pray for Your presence in the Church and in all who seek You.

(Pause for quiet prayer.)

Help us to be a people of integrity and to live what is true.

> **Guide all those who are making their Lenten journey. Deepen in all of us our knowledge and awareness of You.**

Source of our life,

Make us fruitful.

---

3) Abiding God, we pray to live the mystery of wheat that dies and is raised up again.
(Pause for quiet prayer.)

Help us to shoulder the crosses and burdens of our lives.

Give us the grace to trust You even in times of pain and suffering. Help us to lighten the burdens of others.

Source of courage,

Help us to know you better.

---

4) God of Love, we pray that Your law will be written in our hearts.

(Pause for quiet prayer.)

Help us to serve the world with compassion and generosity.

Give us the grace to bring Your renewing spirit to those who suffer. Help us to do justice for the homeless, the neglected, and the outcast.

Source of our mission,

Burn in our hearts.

---

5) Creator God, we pray that You lead the human family away from deeds of hate and anger.

(Pause for quiet prayer.)

Keep us from the works of violence, revenge, and destruction.

Grant Your deepest wisdom to the leaders of the world, especially to those entrusted with the powers of our own nation. Sustain all those who are working for peace and alternatives to violence.

Source of wisdom,

Teach us a new way to live.

---

6) God of Life, we pray that You make us whole in heart and mind, in body and soul.

(Pause for quiet prayer.)

Help us to reach out to those who hunger for consolation and for restoration.

We lift up to you the wounded and the sick, those recovering from surgery, and all those who struggle with every sort of ailment, especially those who are dear to us:

(The assembly speaks aloud the names of the sick.)

Source of healing,

Grant us fullness of life.

---

6) Tender God, we ask You to remember those who experience the mystery of death.

(Pause for quiet prayer.)

Console those who have lost loved ones, and receive into your care those who have passed from this life.

We pray especially for those who have died in acts of violence, neglect, and warfare, and all the dead who are dear to us:

(The assembly speaks aloud the names of the dead.)

Source of eternal life,

Raise us to new life.

---

7) (Option for additional intentions.)

(In closing, the following is prayed by a leader or by all:)

God of constant love,
We offer You our prayers
  this day in faith,
not so as to change You,
but that we ourselves
  may be changed.

Grant us the grace of the seed that surrenders to the earth
and is thus brought to deeper life.

Work in us as You worked
  in Jesus,
for You are our God,
forever and ever. **Amen.**

∎ ∎ ∎

Lenten Scripture Meditations

I do not remember when I was first introduced to the concept of "writing in Scripture mode," but I think that I was formally reintroduced to it in the course of a (Jesuit influenced) directed retreat somewhere in my younger adulthood. In the course of that retreat I was encouraged to allow my imagination (with all its sense-abilities) to enter into Scripture, its settings, situations, and personalities. Since I was a fairly constant journal-keeper at the time, those imaginative inroads became the stuff of writing—dialogues and poems that seemed to liberate Scripture from a more distant experience of intellect-only to a far more felt and personal thing.

The gospel meditations that follow are not intended as theological explanations or textual exegesis. Rather, they are indicators of how one might enter into the people and story of Scripture in such a way as to allow a different kind of insight than the act of "looking at" allows. Looking on the surface of a situation can reveal some things, but stepping into a situation offers a whole different perspective. In these meditations, I allow myself the luxury of the latter perspective, and I am sometimes surprised at how Scripture people and their experience become far more dynamic for me. I also find that in these writings I link much more concretely to the spiritual experience, and the reality of the person having this experience, with the foibles, struggle, and wonder that are often part of the story.

These writings can be used in conjunction with one's own personal prayer, as an inroad for a similar practice for reflection, or they can be interpreted in a prayer service where the particular Scripture reading is used. Each of the pieces has a certain "voice," a "persona" that invites the speaker (these are usually pieces I particularly "hear") to bring to life a Scripture person in a prayer service in a way that is far different from the usual "talking about" mode of preaching. To hear the story from a text and to hear a story from the teller herself are two very different things.

This concept of inhabiting a persona is, of course, related to the power of theatre. People gifted in interpretive reading and in characterizing through voice or gesture can be especially helpful in carrying off these meditations in a group setting. I have worked with folks over the years with these kind of pieces and the experience is usually very rich and illuminating. If one is squeamish about the intersection of "drama" and "prayer," it may be helpful to remember that drama originated in ancient liturgical behavior, and religious drama has a very old root in the life of cathedral communities. Imagination need not be feared. It is as valid an inroad to the Divine as any other human capacity.

A Gospel Meditation in a Lucan Lent

But Who Do You Say That I Am?
DEDICATED TO SISTER PATRICIA SCHNAPP, RSM, WITH GRATITUDE FOR THE INSPIRATION

Once when Jesus was praying in private and his disciples were with him, he asked them, "Who do the crowds say I am?" They replied, "Some say John the Baptist; others say Elijah; and still others, that one of the prophets of long ago has come back to life." "But what about you?" he asked. "Who do you say I am?" (Luke 9:18–20)

It's that annoying question the
   Beloved asks the lover,
   who earnestly picks
   at lint on his jacket
   avoiding a response,
   again.
   But still,
   he pauses, certain that
   the awkward silence
   will finally reveal something.

"There's no good way to answer
   this,"
   the Lenten lover thinks;
   every utterance will
   condemn him
   to an action:
   an embrace,
   an honest kiss,
   a kind of gentle dying that
   lays bare
   the soul's secret,
      unsurrendered, still.

"Could you be a little more
   specific?"
   he asks, buying time,
   seeking shelter
   from eyes that probe with
   knowing,
   but as well with love.

"I'm not sure what you're
   looking for!"
   And he stares heavenward
   awaiting a merciful drop of
   sky
   upon his head, crushing him
   with an excuse for dumbness.

"What was the question?"

And He stands there,
   silent,
   arms folded,
   waiting.
   Maybe
   a little less patient this year,
   maybe
   a little disappointed
   that the cyclic review of that
   Book,
   thorn-pierced,
   wine-stained, and
   steeped in blood,
   seems
   of such small worth.

And the lover,
   now lint-less,
   with a troubled tongue,
   stammers,
   wrestling for words
   he longs to spill into the
   silence,
   and feigns an answer:

"I don't remember…"
   but points to a stubborn
   unconverted
      heart,
   slowly cracking.

■ ■ ■

A Meditation from the Gospel of Luke

The Crippled Woman's Tale

There appeared a woman with a spirit that had crippled her for eighteen years. She was bent over and was quite unable to stand up straight. (Luke 13:11)

This
you may know:
the endless days of downward
    glance
because the hand of God
has weighed heavy
on your spine.

A tree accursed
season after season
makes a crippled arch of
your up-singing youth.
The skyward gaze of your
    childhood
is twisted,
and the world is sideways,
a partial place of silhouettes
and pitying shadows.

Others see horizons,
suns setting and rising.
You see whorls of dust,
the droppings of animals in the
    road,
small plants with shy blooms in
    crevices,
unnoticed,
fallen children
crying for a maternal snatching
from the depths.

The world goes by;
you know people by footfall,
not by face.
Before they greet you,
if they greet you,
you feel their stare
over the curve of your back,
if they see you at all.

It is so easy to almost disappear.

Then,
this
you may not know:
a voice
from a corner of a world
    touching yours.
A touch
of hands
not pushing you out of the way
but, rather,
holding that bent part of
    yourself
and lifting it
to a God who does not curse
but blesses,
so that what was bent
unfurls,
fernlike,
before the faces
that now you see,
all amazed,
incredulous,
and round-mouthed in awe.

And
for a time,
your arms will not stop
their embrace of sun,
their dance above your head,
where your laughter rises
bird-like
in the new sky.

■ ■ ■

A Meditation from the Gospel of John

The One That You Love Is Ill

Now a man named Lazarus was sick. He was from Bethany, the village of Mary and her sister Martha. This Mary, whose brother Lazarus now lay sick, was the same one who poured perfume on the Lord and wiped his feet with her hair. So the sisters sent word to Jesus, "Lord, the one you love is sick." (John 11:1–3)

A long time ago
in a desert land
when dry and heat were
the constant season
and death was the final word
for everything,
there was a people who lived
in perpetual bondage.

A long time ago,
there was a people
with eyes that saw
only a little of the heavens,
with ears that heard
only a portion
    of the world's song,
with lips that spoke
only some of what was true.

A long time ago,
not far from these people,
there was also a Holy Man
who wandered the desert
and the out-of-the-way places
and the wastelands.
And he traveled the whole land
a little alone
so that he might
behold the heavens' lights,
both kind and fierce,
and listen to the world's songs,
both lovely and harsh,
and hear in his heart
the true voice of God,
so that he in turn
might speak it to the people.

One day,
there was
among the people
a friend of the Holy Man
who died
too soon.
And in the custom of the day,
those who mourned
washed in tears
the lifeless body
for a last time,
anointed it
with pungent oils,
and wrapped it
in many layers of linen,
sealing eyes
against the light,
closing ears
against the sound of the world,
strapping shut young lips
frozen
in the shape of the last
    utterance.

And then
thus bound,
they carried the body away
and placed it in a small cave
and rolled a stone
over the entrance,
like the final word
of a brief song.

A few days
too much later,
the Holy Man
came to the grave
seeking one whom he loved.
Guided by the sound
    of mourners
who believed
death
was the final word,
he stood among the people.

Some of them murmured
in clusters amongst the stones,
spitting disbelief
and anger
against the Holy Man.

> "He could have saved…"
> "This life need not
>   have ended…"
> "Why didn't he come
>   sooner?"

But the Holy Man
only walked to the tomb.

"Roll the stone away,"
he said to the people there.

"Ah! but there is only
    death here.
The truth of death!
The stench of the final word!
There is only death
wrapped in linen
and scented with oil..."

"Roll away the stone," he said.

So, reluctantly,
they pressed shoulders to rock,
straining in the heat
to do the bidding of the
strange,
powerful
man.

And the Holy Man
stood like a tree
with arms uplifted
    in the morning sun.
He called out
the name of the one
    who had died.
He called into
the cold stone place,
through the weight
    of final ritual,
beyond the tight linen strips,
past the final word.

He spoke
with power and tenderness
the name of one who
    was bound.
He called
with undeniable authority
that pressed through
the oppressive heat of day:

"LAZARUS. COME OUT!"

A breeze blew
the cool impossibility
    of moisture
past the crowd
and into the tomb.
And from the cradling
    stone ledge
in the shallow dark,
the one who seemed
dead
shuffled,
bound and blind,
to the mouth of the cave,
following the distant
    summoning sound.

The Holy Man
instructed those who were there:
"Unbind this one
who is not dead.
Set my beloved free."

And trembling,
astonished,
shattered,
they set to undo
all that law and grief
had required.

And under a shifting sky,
the bound and the not-bound
felt the granite tonnage
of the final word crack
as the whole world shook
    and tipped towards Bethany.

■ ■ ■

The Spring Transformation

A Meditation from the Gospel of Mark

Seasonal Affective Disorder—The New Demoniac

They went across the lake to the region of the Gerasenes. When Jesus got out of the boat, a man with an evil spirit came from the tombs to meet him. This man lived in the tombs, and no one could bind him any more, not even with a chain. For he had often been chained hand and foot, but he tore the chains apart and broke the irons on his feet. No one was strong enough to subdue him. Night and day among the tombs and in the hills he would cry out and cut himself with stones. When he saw Jesus from a distance, he ran and fell on his knees in front of him. He shouted at the top of his voice, "What do you want with me, Jesus, Son of the Most High God? Swear to God that you won't torture me!" (Mark 5:1–7)

Some people,
we are told,
when September sails
   down
into brown and brittle,
find the failing of the light
a source for senseless sighs,
unfounded,
deep-rooted,
crippling spells of
   funk
over nothing particular.

They plunge into
grave thoughts of the universe
heaving into entropy,
the vacating of stars,
and subtle eclipses of sun and
   soul.

   They suffer some cold lunacy
when November's pewter skies
hang lead-heavy,
their psyches better left
simmering
in July's slow juices,
languid wilted gardens,
fierce cerulean skies,
hammering heat
well into night—
a brief black
more like blue,
but bruised yellow
at the edges.

But it is spring
that has triggered
our many-voiced madness:
the press of iris swords
splitting ground,
the shedding of husks,
velvety,
waxy,
bone-like,
from buds
impatient with winter sleep,
clustered on locust,
willow,
birch—
common trees made
uncommon

in their first airy blush.

Our brittle spirit cringes
as tulips brave
their bloom against the
dying winter sky,
taunting the maybe-snows,
thrusting their prayer for rain
into the air,
thick with new greening.

We cramp.
We panic.
We howl.
Desperate
we cast ourselves
from stone to mud,
trying to hide
from the inevitable eruption
of life
in the midst of our practiced
   death.

Where will we bury our
old, old thoughts—
more at home with cold
that keeps
(as if ice were amber)
emergent insect youth
immobile and entombed?

Where is there to hide
when sun strides
like the harbinger of the Most
    High
near naked,
hatless,
over lawns grown supple,
dandelion dotted,
these fields bent by feet,
playing bare
for the first time?

Where,
if December is departed,
will all that is
unyielding in us
find a changeless refuge?

Son of Man—
herald of a fresher age,
can you quell our rage,
rage at the coming of your light?

We thrash against the invisible
and damn at dawn the chase of
    sun.

Must you send us all into exile
as April feasts on the last frosts?

Must you
summon the beleaguered earth
to break its winter shackles
and sing a sound
so powerful
that our soul's
wild defense
shatters
before your gentle command?

Oh, Son of Spring,
swear you will not torture me
with the green promise
that unmasks every tomb
and untangles
every lie!

■ ■ ■

A Lenten Scripture Service

With the Woman at the Well

APPLICATION

An individual or group prayer for Lent or other appropriate occasion. This service can be expanded in various ways, including a service of reconciliation, renewal of baptismal commitment, or an RCIA retreat, etc. The prayer can be interwoven with music or song.

SET UP

Depending on numbers and location, the service can happen in a circle of chairs around vessels of water or a fountain, or a fitting outdoor setting on retreat or church grounds. An icon/image of the woman at the well may prove helpful as a focus. A worship aid with the texts is necessary (or a PowerPoint equivalent). There are portions for various readers. All read the parts in bold. Projected images of water can also be employed if such a video system is available. Short of a natural feature, sound recordings of water can be used to good effect. There is also one vessel (or more if numbers require) of water for drinking and cups for each participant.

CALL TO PRAYER

As people are gathering, an extended recording of water might be played. Various (clear) containers of water can be brought to the center space and poured into a larger vessel. Prayer could begin with a call to mindfulness (quiet, intentional breathing or appropriate music or song).

CALL TO PRAYER/ GATHERING

(People assemble to the soundtrack of water [possibly progressive: dripping water, brook, stream, waterfall, ocean surf].)

Leader: The refreshment, renewal, and life of the Spirit is with you!

All: And it's with you too.

Leader: My friends,
welcome to this place and time
   that are made holy by
   our intention and the Spirit
   of Jesus.

We know that the gospels are
   full of experiences
in which seekers who meet Jesus
   of Nazareth
   undergo profound change
   from their encounter.

We might also perceive that
   Jesus himself is changed
as he engages with people
   whose need, boldness,
   or faith
push past the boundaries
   of social and religious
   convention
into the realm of conversion
   and changed world views.

Today we turn our attention to
   a very important meeting
   between

Jesus and the mysterious
and bold woman
at a well, in the middle
of the day,
in the middle of two
experiences of thirst.

As we engage this gospel,
let's be open to the thirst that
may be within us
and the presence of the One
who answers that thirst.

Together, let us pray:

**ALL: O God of Deepest Life,
the heart of Jesus was opened
with the bold faith of
the Samaritan woman
at the well.
Her heart was opened
by the new vision he had
for her life.
Open us now with
Your tender strength,
Your mercy,
and the power of
Your living Word.**

**Transform all those
who honestly seek You
into Your loving vision
for us,
through Christ our Lord.
Amen.**

THE PROCLAMATION OF HOLY SCRIPTURE

The First Reading:
Exodus 17:1–7
(*All read the portions in bold.*)

A Reading from the Book of Exodus.

From the wilderness of sin the whole congregation of the Israelites journeyed by stages, as the Lord commanded. They camped at Rephidim, but there was no water for the people to drink. The people quarreled with Moses, and said, **"Give us water to drink."** Moses said to them, "Why do you quarrel with me? Why do you test the Lord?" But the people thirsted there for water; and the people complained against Moses and said, **"Why did you bring us out of Egypt, to kill us and our children and livestock with thirst?"** So Moses cried out to the Lord, "What shall I do with this people? They are almost ready to stone me." The Lord said to Moses, "Go on ahead of the people, and take some of the elders of Israel with you; take in your hand the staff with which you struck the Nile, and go. I will be standing there in front of you on the rock at Horeb. Strike the rock, and water will come out of it, so that the people may drink." Moses did so, in the sight of the elders of Israel. He called the place Massah and Meribah, because the Israelites quarreled and tested the Lord, saying, "Is the Lord among us or not?"

Here is the word that saves.

Thanks be to God.

(*There is a period of silence to reflect on the following questions: What resonates for you in the reading? What caught your eye, your ear, your heart?*)

The Responsorial:
Psalm 95 (*or appropriate music*)

(*All read the parts in bold type.*)

Come, let us sing to the Lord; let us shout for joy to the Rock of our salvation.

Let us come before God's presence with thanksgiving and raise a loud shout to the Most High with psalms.

For our God is a great God, and a great Sovereign above all gods.

The Spring Transformation

The Holy One holds the caverns of the earth, and sustains the heights of the hills.

The sea belongs to God, who made it, whose hands have molded the dry land.

Come, let us bow down, and bend the knee, and kneel before the Lord our Maker.

For the Everlasting One is our God, and we are the people of God's pasture, and the sheep of God's hand.

Oh, that today we would hearken to God's voice!

Let us harden not our hearts, as our ancestors did in the wilderness, at Meribah, and on that day at Massah, when they tempted God.

They put the Almighty to the test, though they had seen God's works.

Forty long years God detested that generation and said, "This people are wayward in their hearts; they do not know my ways."

So the Almighty swore in wrath, "They shall not enter into my rest."

THE GOSPEL READING:
John 4:5–42
(One reader reads the parts in regular type, another the parts in italics, and the congregation the parts in bold—women or men or all, as indicated.)

A reading of the holy Gospel of Our Lord Jesus Christ according to John.

Open our ears and hearts, O God.

So [Jesus] came to a Samaritan city called Sychar, near the plot of ground that Jacob had given to his son Joseph. Jacob's well was there, and Jesus, tired out by his journey, was sitting by the well. It was about noon. A Samaritan woman came to draw water, and Jesus said to her, *"Give me a drink."* (His disciples had gone to the city to buy food.)

The Samaritan woman said to him, *[women]* **"How is it that you, a Jew, ask a drink of me, a woman of Samaria?"** (Jews do not share things in common with Samaritans.) Jesus answered her, *"If you knew the gift of God, and who it is that is saying to you, 'Give me a drink,' you would have asked him, and he would have given you living water."* The woman said to him, *[women]* **"Sir, you have no bucket, and the well is deep. Where do you get that living water? Are you greater than our ancestor Jacob, who gave us the well, and with his sons and his flocks drank from it?"**

Jesus said to her, *"Everyone who drinks of this water will be thirsty again, but those who drink of the water that I will give them will never be thirsty. The water that I will give will become in them a spring of water gushing up to eternal life."* The woman said to him, *[women]* **"Sir, give me this water, so that I may never be thirsty or have to keep coming here to draw water."** Jesus said to her, *"Go, call your husband, and come back."* The woman answered him, *[women]* **"I have no husband."** Jesus said to her, *"You are right in saying, 'I have no husband'; for you have had five husbands, and the one you have now is not your husband. What you have said is true!"* The woman said to him *[women]*, **"Sir, I see that you are a prophet. Our ancestors worshiped on this mountain, but you say that the place where people must worship is in Jerusalem."**

Jesus said to her, *"Woman, believe me, the hour is coming when you will worship the Father neither on this mountain nor in Jerusalem.*

You worship what you do not know; we worship what we know, for salvation is from the Jews. But the hour is coming, and is now here, when the true worshipers will worship the Father in spirit and truth, for the Father seeks such as these to worship him. God is spirit, and those who worship him must worship in spirit and truth." The woman said to him *[**women**]*, **"I know that the Messiah is coming"** (who is called Christ). **"When he comes, he will proclaim all things to us."** Jesus said to her, *"I am he, the one who is speaking to you."*

Just then his disciples came. They were astonished that he was speaking with a woman, but no one said, *[**men**]* **"What do you want?" "Why are you speaking with her?"**

Then the woman left her water jar and went back to the city. She said to the people, *[**women**]* **"Come and see a man who told me everything I have ever done! He cannot be the Messiah, can he?"** They left the city and were on their way to him. Meanwhile the disciples were urging him, *[**men**]* **"Rabbi, eat something."** But he said to them, *"I have food to eat that you do not know about."* So the disciples said to one another, *[**men**]* **"Surely no one has brought him something to eat?"** Jesus said to them, *"My food is to do the will of him who sent me and to complete his work. Do you not say, 'Four months more, then comes the harvest'? But I tell you, look around you, and see how the fields are ripe for harvesting. The reaper is already receiving wages and is gathering fruit for eternal life, so that sower and reaper may rejoice together. For here the saying holds true, 'One sows and another reaps.' I sent you to reap that for which you did not labor. Others have labored, and you have entered into their labor."*

Many Samaritans from that city believed in him because of the woman's testimony, *[**women**]* **"He told me everything I have ever done."** So when the Samaritans came to him, they asked him to stay with them; and he stayed there two days. And many more believed because of his word. They said to the woman, *[**all**]* **"It is no longer because of what you said that we believe, for we have heard for ourselves, and we know that this is truly the Savior of the world."**

The Gospel of the Lord.

ALL: Praise to you, Lord Jesus Christ.

(There is a period of silence to reflect on the following questions: What resonates for you in the reading? What caught your eye, your ear, your heart?)

GROUP REFLECTION
(Or prepared reflection)

(We share what we heard in our hearts and heads in the readings and in the silence.)

PRAYERS OF THE PEOPLE: THE NAMING OF THIRSTS

LEADER: Let us pray for the needs of our lives, our communities, our planet:

1) God of Creation, we live on a thirsty planet.

> **Water is scarce
>   in many places.
> Our oceans, seas, and lakes
>   we have poisoned.
> Drought touches many
>   parts of the globe.**

Pour out Your saving rains,

> **And answer
>   our constant thirst.**

2) God of the Heavens, we live in thirsty times.

> **Many peoples
>   are parched for peace.
> We need the restoration of
>   our global relationships.**

The Spring Transformation

**The Earth cracks where
 violence dries up our
 various resources.**

Pour out Your saving rains,

**And answer
 our constant thirst.**

3) God With Us, we walk a long journey in the desert.

**We are often weary
 for want of refreshment.
We grow impatient
 with the path we take
 with You.
Our thirst claws from
 the inside when we
 are scared.**

Pour out Your saving rains,

**And answer
 our constant thirst.**

4) Holy One, like our ancestors in faith, we need Your presence.

**Our hearts grow weary
 when apart from You.
Our souls cry out
 with the deepest needs.
In our wandering our
 isolation sharpens our
 craving for You.**

Pour out Your saving rains,

**And answer
 our constant thirst.**

5) Lord of Deep Waters, like the woman at the well, we reach out to You.

**Our curiosity about
 You compels us
  to draw near to You.
Our journeys bring us
 to You, for the world
 cannot supply
 our need.
Our deep thirst for
 the water You offer so
 freely makes us bold.**

Pour out Your saving rains,

**And answer
 our constant thirst.**

(Other petitions may be offered.)

Leader:
Lord Jesus,
Our inner thirsts, however
 strong or discomforting,
are blessings when they draw us
 to the well
from which Your
 living water flows.

Help us to be attentive to
 the needs of our souls
and to be ready to find
 You wherever You are
 reaching out to us
in our daily lives.

May Your Spirit lead us
 in our deserts
to the places where

You are waiting for us.

Amen.

A RITE OF WATER

Invitation
My friends,
the water we drink each day
 refreshes us,
keeps our bodies and our brains
 in working order,
and sustains our life
 in this world.
Without water
we cannot last for very long
 at all; we would perish
  without it.

In receiving the water
 here today,
let us remember how this gift
 of the natural world
reminds us of the gift
 of the spiritual world
that also sustains, restores,
 and renews our inner life.
Let us be mindful of that water
 without which we would
  perish within.

As you "come to the well"
 for a drink,
I invite you to consciously
 carry with you
the particular thirst that
 you have today
and be open to the grace
 that may answer that
  thirst in your life
at this moment.

WE COME TO THE WATER
(People come forward and receive clear, cool water. This can be done in several ways:

1. *A leader pours water for each person who comes forward.*
2. *In relay, a leader starts the process of pouring water and each in turn pours water for the next.*
3. *People draw their own water from a vessel with a dipper.)*

(Appropriate music is played or sung during the above—e.g., "Water of Life" [Haas], or "Come to the Water" [Foley]. There is a period of quiet reflection after the water rite.)

COMMUNAL PRAYER

Holy One,
Maker and sustainer
 of us all,
we thank You for the water
 that keeps us alive
  each day
and the deep water
 that keeps our souls
  alive in You.
We also thank You
 for the company we
  have kept in this time,
and the inspiration
 of our hearts and minds.

In the (Lenten) days
 that are still before us,
especially when we
 encounter stretches
  of dry desert,
we ask You
 to keep us faithful
and to pour out in us
 the water that gives
  eternal life,
from the well of which
 You are the generous
  source.

Keep us always mindful
 of Your presence,
and be with us in
 our transformation
through love and grace,
 through Christ
  our Lord.
AMEN.

FINAL BLESSING AND DISMISSAL

LEADER:
From the desert of broken
 relationships and the dry
 lands of spiritual searching,
through the waters
 of our renewal,
may we be true to the One who
 calls us to deeper life.

And may God bless us all, God
who Creates, Christ who Saves,
and the Spirit who Sanctifies.

AMEN.

Our prayer and reflection
 have ended.
Refreshed by the Spirit
let us go now into the world
 in peace.

Thanks be to God.

(Optional song or sign of peace or sprinkling.)

■ ■ ■

A Service for Healing and Forgiveness

With the Paralyzed Man

BACKGROUD

Nearly one-fifth of the gospels is dedicated to the healing ministry of Jesus. Many of the Lenten stories refer to Jesus bringing health and wholeness to those who believed in him. Healing and restoration are key to the journey of Lent.

APPLICATION

A service for Lent, a retreat, or other appropriate occasion. This service can be expanded in various ways, including a service of reconciliation, a healing service, or an RCIA retreat, etc. The prayer can be interwoven with music or song.

SET UP

A reflective space with a simple, draped table with small bowls of oil (appropriate for the size of the assembly) and a candle. Private spaces for the sacrament of reconciliation (or "holy listening") are ready before the service. An icon of Christ that expresses forgiveness and acceptance is useful for setting an environment of reflection. Simple stick incense (sandalwood or other cleansing scent) burning from a bowl of sand or earth can also underscore a sense of healing, prayer, or transformation.

The assembly reads all parts in bold type, so a printed text is needed for the assembly. This can be in a worship aid of some sort or rendered as PowerPoint slides with images or color.

CALL TO PRAYER

As people are gathering, soft music may be played. A quiet ambience for reflection and prayerfulness is helpful.

CALL TO PRAYER

(We are invited to be mindful of God's presence as we breathe three deep breaths together. Option for song based on Psalm 130, e.g., "Out of the Depths" [Soper], or "Remember Your Love" [Balhoff, Ducote, Daigle].)

GREETING AND REMEMBRANCE OF GOD'S MERCY

Leader:
The renewing grace
and the tender mercy
of God Our Maker
be with you all.

All: And also with you.

Leader:
My friends, we are gathered here to remember once again that God's presence is among us, eager to heal, forgive, and restore us. As we continue our Lenten journey of renewal, we do so in a time when the world remains noisy with the sounds of battle, swallowed up in its perpetual struggles. Especially in the midst of such conflict, it is good for us to be mindful of the covenant God has with us and to recall that the mercy of God is extended to all peoples. Let us take a moment of silence to recall those areas in the world,

in our own lives, and in the lives of those we love that are in need of healing and restoration.

(There is a substantial silence. People may be invited to kneel. The following litany may also use a sung Kyrie/Lord Have Mercy response.)

Creating God,
You are greater than
   we can comprehend.
Your power shapes the universe.
You give breath to all life.

**God have mercy!
God have mercy on us all!**

Loving God,
Your touch brings healing.
You hold us when we
   are broken.
You bring us life,
   even out of death.

**God have mercy!
God have mercy on us all!**

Spirit God,
You are the force of change
   and renewal.
You have hope for humankind.
You make possible what
   we cannot imagine.

**God have mercy!
God have mercy on us all!**

Let us pray together:

ALL:

**O God of mercy
   and compassion,
here in this Lenten season,
   we know that within us
     there is much
that resists transformation,
much that struggles
   to surrender,
and much that still resists
   Your invitation
     to be healed.
We ask in our prayer today
that You open us up
   to the voice
     and presence of Jesus,
so that we might be drawn
   more deeply
into the conversion that
   we most long for.**

We pray in the name of the Christ, Your Son our Lord, who listened closely to You and lived Your way, Loving God, forever and ever. AMEN.

GOSPEL READING:

Matthew 9:1–8

READER: *(before reading)* This is a reading of the Good News according to Matthew:

(after the reading) Let those with ears to hear now hear.

ALL: Thanks be to God.

OPTIONAL SHARED RESPONSE TO THE GOSPEL READING

(Or prepared reflections)

(Following the reflection, there is a period of quiet or an appropriate song.)

A LITANY FOR HEALING

LEADER: My friends, let us lift our voices to God and ask for healing for ourselves, our land, and the peoples of the Earth. Please stand.

God of Wholeness, we live in
   a wounded time.
Sickness and shadow touch our
   lives, our land, our souls.
Hear our prayers this day,
   for ourselves
     and for our planet.
They come from our hearts,
   with an earnest desire
     for healing.

(The following may be led by assigned readers or be read antiphonally by the assembly.)

1) Let us pray for all believing peoples. *(pause)*

From wounds of division,
from blindness of spirit,
from hardness of heart,
from belief that we have
   all the answers,

from hypocrisy in all its forms,
and from lethargy,
we pray to You, O God:

Heal us and make us whole.

2) Let us pray for those who
govern nations and powers,
especially in this difficult time.
(pause)

From the urge to want
    too much,
from blindness to the needs
    of the poor and voiceless,
from the cancer of too much
    power and wealth,
from the desire for warfare
    and control by violence,
from our fear of community
    and our resistance to change,
we pray to You, O God:

Heal us and make us whole.

3) Let us pray for our own
country, for all who lead, follow,
and serve. *(pause)*

From the disorders
    of consumption and greed,
from demons of rage
    and crippling violence,
from fear of new ways
    of being and doing,
from dementia that keeps us
    from the truth of ourselves,
from vision too narrow,
    and disbelief in our power
    to choose,
we pray to You, O God:

Heal us and make us whole.

4) Let us pray for those who are
not well. *(pause)*

From diseases that harm
    the body and ailments
        that weaken the mind,
from insults to the soul and self,
from wounds from long ago
    and injuries sustained
        this day,
from fatigue for those
    who care for the ill,
from depression, addiction,
    compulsion, despair, and
        all cripplings of the spirit,
and for those whom we name
    aloud at this time
        who need healing:
*(We name those who need
healing.)*
We pray to You, O God:

Heal us and make us whole.

5) Let us remember those who
are dying. *(pause)*

From the terror of death,
from fear of letting go,
from abandonment
    at the final hour,
from amnesia about the total
    mercy of Our Maker,
we pray to You, O God:

Heal us and make us whole.

6) Let us remember those who
have died. *(pause)*

From our forgetfulness
    of the good done by others
        in our lives,
from our fear for their welfare
    in the life to come,
from our reticence to forgive
    and release,
for our wounded trust
    in the God who loves us all,
and for those who have died
whom we name aloud
    at this time:
(We name those who have died.)
We pray to You, O God:

Heal us and make us whole.

Holy One, Lover of us all,
See in us our desire for
    wholeness for ourselves
        and all our world.
Help us to find healing—
    to receive both Your
        divine aid
and the grace to heal ourselves.
We make our prayer
    through Your Great Spirit,
You who love humanity
    and seek to make it whole.

AMEN.

A RITE OF ANOINTING

Leader *(in these or similar words)*:

From very ancient times and in many cultures, anointing with oil has been used for blessing, cleansing, designation of special service like priesthood or kingship, and for the work of healing.

In our prayer today, aware of the role that we each play in this community in aiding the healing of our brothers and sisters, we will sign one another with the oil in these bowls on our foreheads and on the palms of the hands.

As you sign one another with the oil, I invite you to say: "May the Lord heal you of every ailment of heart, mind, and body." And I invite the person who is being anointed to reply: "I accept the healing touch of the One who calls me."

(The assembly proceeds to administer the oil. Appropriate music may be played/sung to accompany the action. When all is done, there is a period of silence.)

CLOSING PRAYER

Leader: Let us stand and pray together.

All:
**Holy One, lover of us all,
see in us our earnest desire
  for ourselves and
  all our world
to become whole.**

**Open the infected wounds
  we hide from You.
Straighten the jagged scars
  on our hearts
  and psyches.
Heal the diseases that
  remain fiercely hidden
  from our own eyes
and lay them bare in the
  restoring light
  of Your Son.**

**Help us to be open to the
voice, the touch, the love
of Your life in us.**

**We make our prayer
  through the Spirit
  of Your Christ,
Jesus, who loved humanity
  and sought to
  make it whole.**

Amen.

(Closing song or sign of peace.)

■ ■ ■

The Spring Transformation

A Lenten Table Prayer

For Healing

APPLICATION

A gathering during Lent. Works well for an alternative sabbath gathering, parish meeting, family gathering, retreat, ecumenical gathering of several communities, etc. This prayer form lends itself to a potluck meal. Given the Lenten setting, a simple meal of bread and soup may be fitting. The prayer can be prayed on its own or combined with a Scripture reading and reflection, as time and numbers allow.

SET UP

This is prayed by a group gathered around a single (expanded) table or at a series of tables. Tables can be set as simply or as elaborately as resources allow. Candlelight and tablecloths are conducive to the sense of a ceremonial meal. Lengths of purple material on tables are expressive in themselves.

At the table, all have a copy of the text and a glass. The fruit of the vine (wine or juice) is distributed to each person's glass, or there can be a more deliberate ritualizing of its pouring within the prayer itself. A loaf of bread for breaking is in readiness at a leader's place, or a loaf of bread can be present at each table.

Individuals read the numbered portions (this can be designated in advanced or done at table, spontaneously). All read the parts in bold.

CALL TO PRAYER

The meal begins with an indication of the nature of the prayer, a word about the focus on healing in the season of Lent, and some sort of call to mindfulness (quiet, intentional breathing or meditational music or song). A designated leader lights a candle and begins the prayer when all are ready.

INTRODUCTION

God of all seasons and times,
be with Your people.

**Source of our being,
be with us here.**

Saving Christ,
healer of body and soul,
be among us.

**Let us hear Your voice
and know You.**

Holy Spirit, our breath of life,

**Move among us anew
and draw us to You.**

Peace be with you all.

And also with you!

My friends, as we enter into
our Lenten table prayer,
let us take a moment of quiet
to consider the wounds we bear
and the power of our God to heal:

(There is a period of silence. We consider what we bring to the table, what needs healing.)

God our Beloved, source of every blessing, Your healing care is extended to us every day. No matter our wounds and failings, by the work of Your Spirit, lead us to receive Your restoring grace and to acknowledge Your gift with joy, through Christ our Lord. **AMEN.**

A LITANY OF ACKNOWLEDGMENT

Leader: My friends, we know full well that we bear wounds within ourselves. We are also conscious that our communities locally and globally also bear wounds and are diseased in different ways. The beginning of healing is an acknowledgment that something is not whole. Let us name now what needs the touch of God.

1) **God of mercy, heal the fragmented Church!**

In the power of Your Word,
in the sharing of our mission,
in the breaking of the Bread,

> **Make us whole
> and a sign of love.**

2) **God of creation, heal our embattled and poisoned world!**

In the peace of compassionate
   thinking and doing,
in the power of wisdom
   of inspired action,
in the glory of all humans
   fully alive, together,

> **Make us whole
> and a work of love.**

3) **God of justice, heal our fractured nation!**

In leadership born of service,
in communities that help
   the poor,
in families of all kinds,
   all struggling, all caring,

> **Make us whole
> and a people of love.**

4) **God of human hearts, heal our broken relationships!**

Through time shared tenderly,
through words shared honestly,
through minds and souls open
   to forgiveness,

> **Make us whole
> and a community of love.**

5) **God of Jesus Christ, heal us, body and soul!**

Those who suffer isolation,
   depression, and addiction,
those who suffer from chronic
   pain, grief, and mourning,
those who endure illness
   and injury,
and those we recall at this time:

(We name aloud those who need healing.)

6) **God of eternal life, bring us to our everlasting home!**

Those who are dying this hour,
   perhaps forgotten or alone,
those who die in warfare and
   acts of violence,
those who have died confident
   of Your promise,
and those we recall at this time:

(We name aloud those who have died.)

7) Option for additional petitions.

Leader: Let us pray together:

All: Receive these prayers we speak aloud, O God, the prayers we speak in our hearts, and the prayers for which we have no words at all. Help us to trust in You and to see that You are acting in our lives each day with healing grace and tenderness. Through Christ Our Lord. Amen.

PRAYER FOR HEALING

My friends, God is with us!

> **God is with us indeed.**

In trust, let us lift up our hearts!

> **Even with the weight
> of their wounds,
> we lift them up.**

How shall we give thanks to the One who heals us?

The Spring Transformation

**With our voices,
with our aching hearts,
with bread and fruit
of the vine.**

1) Blessed are You, beloved God, for in Your mercy You make us whole.

> **From wounds that we carry
> within and without,
> from afflictions of body
> and soul,
> You set us free.**

2) You reach out in tenderness.

> **You touch with love
> and power.
> Your grace washes over us
> and draws us into deeper life.**

3) Though we often are afraid of Your gifts,

> **Still You are always
> reaching out to us.**

4) Though we place so many conditions on You,

> **Still You call us to respond
> in freedom.**

5) Though our maladies weaken our resolve and challenge our hope,

> **Still You invite us
> to move into
> fullness of life with You.**

6) Your Christ makes whole a people who live crippled in fear and uncertainty.

> **Your Word announces
> the Good News of our
> redemption and health.**

7) For all the ways You heal us, Loving God, we give You thanks and praise.

> **Most of all, we thank
> You for Jesus,
> who with the power of love
> heals our wounds
> and sets us free.**

(Option for an appropriate song of praise.)

8) Creator God, we do thank You for the life of Jesus, Your Son.

> **For his words spoken
> in our isolation,
> for his presence found
> in our loneliness,
> for his power to heal
> our deepest wounds.**

9) We ask that Your Holy Spirit be with us here as we bless and share these gifts of bread and wine—we who are the wounded body of Christ.

> **May that same Spirit
> come upon each of us anew,
> that we may be further
> transformed and healed
> to work more ably as
> the body of Christ
> in the world.**

10) We are gathered in his name, Most High,

> **and we celebrate
> in the manner
> that was handed down to us
> throughout the centuries
> in this banquet
> of our restoration.**

(The bread is lifted up in blessing.)

11) From of old, Your people have offered up the gifts of Your own giving, the grain of the field by which we are fed and sustained.

> **We bless You, Most High,
> for all the ways
> we are nourished,
> for all the ways You keep us
> alive and well.**

Let us take and eat this bread for the health of our body and the strength of our spirits.

(Bread is broken, shared, and eaten by all.)

(The cups are lifted up in blessing.)

12) From of old, Your people have offered up the gifts of Your own giving, the fruit of the vine by which we are delighted and refreshed.

**We bless You, Most High,
for all the ways our thirst
   is answered,
for all the ways You delight
   us and make us glad.**

Let us take and drink this fruit of the vine, for the health of our body and the joy of our hearts.

(The wine/juice is tasted by all.)

13) Holy God, creator of the universe, gathered at this table, we gratefully remember that the wholeness given through Christ is a health for all the world.

**Send Your Holy Spirit
   on us all and heal us
   from every wound
      and ailment:
   from injuries of shame
      and abuse,
   from maladies of pride
      and anger,
   from cancers of flesh
      and spirit.**

14) We ask that Your Spirit may always work to renew us with Your grace.

**Together with
   all Your people,
with the holy and human
   ones who came
      before us,
and with those who will
   come after us,
may we honor You with
our words and deeds,
and praise You for Your gift
   of healing given
      in Christ Jesus.**

15) May our Lenten journey together open us further to the healing power of Jesus, so that we who bear his name may bear witness to his continued presence in the world.

**May our blessing
   of bread and cup
honor his memory
and help us to be
instruments of his healing
   love and forgiveness,
wherever we are led.**

16) For now, as always, we pray together in his saving name.

Amen.

■ ■ ■

The Spring Transformation

A Spring Examen

APPLICATION

An examen is an ancient Church practice that received special focus from Saint Ignatius of Loyola in conjunction with the *Spiritual Exercises*. It presents a programmatic way of looking at one's life in the context of daily reality. The examen below is offered for a seasonal review, considering the natural turn of things and the interior movements that may (or may not) be in harmony with the changes that are often around us, subtle or overt. We are invited to take notice.

SET UP

This can be done with a small group, but more likely fits an individual meditation. It is well matched with a walk of mindfulness (or a set of walks over time) in which one can take concerted effort to be open to what nature is doing. The questions of the examen allow for specific naming of physical and internal changes, the identification of God's presence, and the expression of gratitude.

CALL TO PRAYER

The meditation begins by calling to mind the presence of God, the awakening of the senses, and, as always, mindfulness of breath. A journal is helpful, but any mode of writing is useful.

THE EXAMEN PROCESS

Part 1
I take a leisurely walk, or find a place where I can observe the natural world reflectively.

Part 2
I pay attention to my breathing. I invite God's presence into my meditation.

Part 3
I spend time with the following:
What do I notice around me?
What do I notice within me?
Where do I feel a stirring?
Where do I feel hope for the future?
Where/how do I sense God's presence?
Where do I need the energy of God in this season?

Part 4
For what/whom am I grateful?

CLOSING PRAYER

Gracious One,
once again
I am amazed how time
works its miracle of
transformation.

How does this happen?
These changes,
these eruptions of the earth,
these tiny victories of green
and new births?

Who is the orchestrator
of all this newly released sound?

Who commands these
daggers of color
to cut through the cold
and vanquish it?

Who taught the soil to sing,
and who instructed the trees to
take on this most precious
    green?

And though in mid-winter,
I felt the horrible press of Old,
how is it that now
I am suddenly young,
and all my years are like
illusions found in clouds?

Thank You
again and again,
re-Creator of the world.
My eyes are learning
    to open again.
My ears are relearning to hear.
My heart beats
    with newer beats.
And I am ready.

Amen.

Part II

WELCOME HOLY SPRINGTIDE

Holy Week Prayers and Services

With its nearly daily opportunities for liturgical observances in the Church, Holy Week is the richest (and potentially most exhausting) week in the liturgical calendar. In no other week does the Christian Church have so many varied and expansive ways to examine, embrace, and celebrate the key story of its identity. With Scripture, music, story, and symbol, there is the ritual opportunity to plunge deeply into the mystery of life, death, and resurrection through the experience of Jesus of Nazareth.

This same religious calendar is connected to the timeless agrarian calendar of the earth. Here are the ancient mysteries of survival, death, and renewal that have composed the cycle of human existence (and its rituals) for millennia. Nature provides a certain matrix for religious language, and religious understanding is reinforced by the movements of nature.

The formal liturgies of the Christian Church are manifold for this passage. They have evolved over centuries and reflect geographic, historical, and theological movements. For numbers of people, these Holy Week liturgies represent deep memories and associations with church communities. Many others have never experienced the paschal mystery celebrations outside of the hubbub, crowds, and animation of Easter Sunday. Still others may be looking for new ways to reflect upon and ritualize the paschal mystery.

The offerings here for Holy Week provide a framework for communal and personal entrance into the Great Story. Communal services are presented in particular for communities that may not have a primary priest/minister to lead. Music might be provided by available talent, or well-known pieces from hymn repertoire can be sung by the assembly a cappella.

These services may also make use of spaces in churches that are not typically part of the worship environment. The Holy Week stories are dynamic and are possibly better served by our more overt movement and the shaking up of our traditional patterns and places of worship and prayer. In recalling all of the gospels, but the passion/death/resurrection sequences especially, a sense of place is significant for our comprehension of the dramatic engagement of empire and reign of God, the powers of earth and the powers of heaven (and nature). Sometimes we do not see those source stories, let alone really take in their energy. Sometimes moving things around a bit in our ritual life can wake us up.

Passion/Palm Sunday:

A Walking Service Commemorating the Lord's Entrance into Jerusalem, his Passion, and his Death on the Cross with the Gospel of Mark

APPLICATION

Palm Sunday ecumenical Agape service, Holy Week retreat, RCIA experience, etc. The service below can be lay-led or use available clergy.

BACKGROUND

Palm Sunday sets the stage for Holy Week in many ways. Various liturgical communities may observe only the entrance into Jerusalem in this celebration. Others may blend elements of the entrance with the passion, death, and burial of Jesus in a complex liturgy called Palm/Passion Sunday. The service below endeavors to diminish the wordiness of many similar services, matching action and song with Scriptural story.

In Catholic communities, Lent and Good Friday are frequently the times for the praying of the Stations of the Cross, which have their roots in Crusades times when the faithful were encouraged to make a pilgrimage to the Holy Land and walk the Via Dolorosa (literally, the way of sorrows: the way of the cross). Since that voyage was so prohibitive, the Stations of the Cross developed as a devotional (with its characteristic walk around the church side aisles, ambulatory, or churchyard) with painted or sculpted images of the last journey of Jesus. Instead of looking at artistic scenes, this service invites us to meditate and be "in the scene."

SET UP

As weather permits, people gather outside the church or in a space different from the main worship space. Palm branches are available for distribution to each person in the assembly.

CALL TO PRAYER

Someone welcomes people and explains briefly the meaning and the general flow of the liturgy, its expanded physical path.

WELCOME AND CALL TO PRAYER

BLESSING OF THE PALM BRANCHES AND PROCESSION

(Presider/leader blesses the palms in these or similar words.)

My friends, I invite you now to
lift the palm branches you carry
as we prepare to bless them for
our use.

(The congregation lifts up the palms for the blessing.)

Let us pray:
Creator God, we ask You
   to bless these branches,
and all those who bear them,

(Option: presider/leader sprinkles the branches or makes the sign of the cross.)

and make them holy for our
remembrance and our use today
and in our homes.

Today we joyfully acclaim Jesus
   as our Messiah
as we echo the words and song
   of ancient Jerusalem.

As we open up the doors
   of our church home
     for his entrance today,
so too may we open our hearts

Welcome Holy Springtide

and minds to his words
and to the mystery
    of our salvation.
In doing all this, may we be
    made more ready
        for the New Jerusalem,
the glory of God's holy city,
led by him who lives
    and reigns forever and ever.
AMEN.

Let us listen to the story of the Jesus' entrance into the city of Jerusalem as told in the Gospel of Mark.

GOSPEL READING
Mark 11:1–11

PROCESSION

(Led by banner, icon, or cross, the people, with palm branches uplifted, process around the block or the church and then move inside the building to the space for the Last Supper portion of the service.

As people process, music options might include: "The King of Glory Comes," "All Glory, Praise, and Honor," "Let the King of Glory Come," "Ride On King Jesus," etc. If children are part of the procession, banners that they have made or a gathering of percussion instruments may be welcome.)

REMEMBRANCE OF THE LORD'S LAST SUPPER

(In the Last Supper space, the congregation assembles around chairs placed at an expanded table [or other appropriate setting as numbers dictate] as singing continues until all are present.)

PRESIDER/LEADER:
My friends, we have entered
    our sacred site,
with Jesus, the Son of Promise,
    our healer and teacher.
He is the Christ for whom
    the human family hungers
    and thirsts.

Now, we have left the noise
    of acclamation and joy,
and we turn our hearts
    and minds more quietly
to the one who nourishes us
    as no other.

Let us listen closely to the story
    of Jesus' last days.
Let us be mindful of the people
    who were there with him
as he prepared for his great
    encounter with the empire
and embraced fully his calling.

THE ANOINTING AT BETHANY

READER: Mark 14:1–9

(After the reading recalling the anointing of Jesus, the congregation is anointed with scented oil on palms and forehead. This can be done by appointed persons, or by the whole assembly to one another in relay fashion. Appropriate instrumental music or sung song is an option. Godspell's "By My Side" would be very moving at this time.)

THE LAST SUPPER

(The reading for the following portion may be done by a single reader, several readers, or readers and assembly, as numbers and space allow.)

THE PREPARATION

READER: Mark 14:12–16)

(After this reading, the table is prepared with cloth, bread, fruit of the vine, candles, and flowers. Appropriate music accompanies the action. When all is done, the reading continues.)

Reader: Mark 14:17–22

(After this reading, a leader lifts the bread in blessing and breaks it. The bread is shared around in a manner that befits numbers and space. If numbers are few, this can be done in quiet. If numbers are larger, music may be needed. When all have eaten, the reading continues.)

Reader: Mark 14:23–25

(After this reading, a leader pours out the fruit of the vine in a cup and lifts it in blessing. The wine/juice is shared around in a manner that befits numbers and space. If numbers are few, this can be done in quiet. If numbers are larger, music may be needed. When all have drunk, the reading continues.)

Reader: Mark 14:26

(An appropriate song is sung that dovetails into people's movement into the next space, perhaps with candlelight. If there is no change of space, the meal elements may be cleared away in preparation for the next portion of the gospel.)

THE AGONY IN THE GARDEN, BETRAYAL, AND ARREST

(The "garden" space may be outdoors, an area with some appropriate house plants, or a space with an icon and stands for candles that were carried in procession [or people may hold them through this next portion]. The reading may be passed around the group at each portion, or prepared by appointed readers. The text may be punctuated with appropriate music/song.)

Reader: Mark 14:32–50

THE TRIAL BEFORE THE CHIEF PRIESTS, THE DENIAL OF PETER, AND JESUS BEFORE PILATE

(An appropriate song ["Were You There?" perhaps only hummed] may accompany the people's movement into the next space, with the candlelight from the "garden." In this next space [perhaps the sanctuary], a plain, raw cross is set in place. At the sanctuary, the candle bearers place the candles on stands that are near the cross. Readers continue with the gospel account of the trial of Jesus.)

Reader: Mark 14:53–72

(After the reading, option for music solo: "Sometimes I Feel Like A Motherless Child.")

Reader: Mark 15:1–20

(Music option: "Were You There?" verse 1.)

THE CRUCIFIXION

Reader: Mark 15:21–24

(Music option: "Were You There?" verse 2.)

Reader: Mark 15:25–39

(There is a period of silence.)

Reader: Mark 15:40–41

(Option: the cross is draped with linen cloth, which is carried in by three women.)

Reader: Mark 15:42–47

(Music option: "Were You There?" verse 3.)

(All observe a few moments of silence.)

A PRAYER FOR OPENNESS IN DAYS TO COME

ALL: **Gracious God,**
  (on this holy night)
 at the beginning
  of this Holy Week
  be with us here in light
   and shadow,
  in pain and awe,

in sorrow
    and in humility.

Whatever our creeds,
whatever the songs
    we sing,
whatever our differences
    in belief or deeds,
gather us all together
and help us to be truly
    present in
        this moment
and in the week
    of prayer to come.

Help us to hear
    with new ears
the story that has been
    told for generations.

Help us to receive
    with open hearts
        the gift of Jesus.
Make us receptive
    to the purpose
        and the passion of
the Son of Man,
the seed that fell
    to the ground
so that it would bear
    much fruit.

Give us the grace
    to be continually
        transformed
by the power of love
    that gives the ultimate
        gift.

May our gathering
    this evening
draw us closer to You
    and to Your Christ,
and may it lead us further
    on our own journeys
        in this world,
especially as we encounter
    pain, suffering, and loss.

We make our prayer
through the Spirit and
    in the name of Jesus.

AMEN.

(Music option: "What Wondrous Love Is This?")

(Option: The draped cloth is carefully and gracefully taken off the cross, held aloft, and carried out of the space.)

(All depart quietly.)

■ ■ ■

Monday of Holy Week

An Ecumenical Prayer with the Holy Week Symbols

APPLICATION

For Monday of Holy Week, or Tuesday or Wednesday if there are no other services.

This "crash course" in Holy Week is especially useful for the various ministers that are usually so busy creating Holy Week services that it is difficult for them to graciously enter the spirit and the symbols of each of the days. It can also be a good way to experience the whole of the week's activities with a youth group, family, small faith community, RCIA, etc., in a way that there is room for instructive discussion or reflection before or after the prayer. The prayer can be used without the "stations" of activity as listed below.

SET UP

Works in a single circle for a smaller group with a laying out of the symbols, a larger space with symbols placed up front, or in several stations or spaces of a church or hall. The following stations are used in the prayer:
1) candles in candlesticks
2) basin, pitcher, water, towels
3) bread in basket
4) wine/juice in vessel, single or multiple cups
5) exchange sign of Peace
6) wooden (or other) bowl of substantial nails
7) congregational tapers

There is a worship aid with the text for each person. Music can be used in the background of each "station," or an appropriate song may be sung to accompany the activity if the group is larger. A leader or several readers may be helpful, along with someone to help with the action at each of the "stations."

CALL TO PRAYER

(Can include a teaching on Holy Week, some sort of music, or silent centering.)

PRAYER

(Led by a leader, several readers, or prayed communally or antiphonally. Someone helps lead the actions indicated below.)

My brothers and sisters,
    let us pray:

O Holy One
in these days of remembrance,
as some in our fractious world
turn eyes to the Nazarene,
    and the table,
    and the cross,
    and the tomb,

We ask for the light of grace
    to enter into us,
    to open us to something
    deep,
    lasting,
    and
    transforming.

(We light candles and open our inward eyes.)

Lead us to consider
the mystery
    of a world-changing story,

Welcome Holy Springtide

even as our world
    in this present age
is spewing out its new/old story
of things that never change:
    empires that struggle,
    leaders that grasp,
    people that suffer,
    the innocent that are killed.

In the midst of the chaos that
    does not rest, we ask You:

Give us the mind of the servant,
that we may bend
and tend
and wash
the wounds,
the hands,
the feet of others.

(We wash one another's hands.)

Give us the heart of the hungry,
that we may receive what is
broken for us
and shared
in our need
with
gratitude.

*(We bless and break bread
and share it with each other.)*

Grant us the wisdom
of the thirsty,
that we may receive
with acceptance
what has been
poured for us
and shared
in our need.

(We pour out wine, bless it, pass the cup, and share it with each other.)

Give us the humility
    of those who
have done wrong
    and recognize their fault,
that we may embrace
our blunders,
    our betrayals,
gifts of mercy, and forgiveness.

(We share a sign of peace with each other.)

Give us the strength
    of the suffering,
that we may face
    the horrible things
done in the name of
    governments,
    and religions,
    and business,
    and ideas,
    and in our names,
and who still find reasons
    and ways
    to survive,
    to thrive,
    to love.

(We take a nail from the bowl and remember the suffering of others.)

Grant us the hope of those
   who trust in you,
that we may walk through
   the darkness of Death's
      too-many shadows,
   the uncertainties of our lives,
   and the persecutions that are
   thrust upon
      those who are vulnerable,
      those without voice
         or power,
      the little ones lost
      in the hurry and blur
      of the light-starved world.

(A flame is taken from the table candles and passed, one to another, to the individual candles.)

Let our remembrance
   of the story of Jesus,
      the carpenter's son,
      the teacher of Nazareth,
      the healer of the wounded,
      the challenger of the empire,
      the betrayed,
      the tortured,
      the crucified,
      the buried behind stone,
      the beloved.

Move us each in new ways
   so that something
      may be raised up within us
      to new life.

Open our lips
to utter again with a spring joy
   a word of praise,
   a story of hope,
   a song of wonder,
too long sleeping
in our ashen ground.

AMEN.

A WORD

(This can include an exhortation for ministers serving in Holy Week, an encouragement for people to attend Holy Week Services, or encouragement to embrace the prayerful potential of the week.)

CLOSING

(Option for music, song, or silent departure.)

■ ■ ■

Maundy Thursday

A Service for the Servants

BACKGROUND

Thursday evening of Holy Week begins the great Triduum. In the Roman tradition, there is no formal ending to the Thursday or Friday liturgies. The evening service (beginning like the Jewish prayers at or past sundown) is also known as Maundy Thursday, after the Latin word *mandatum* (command), which refers to Jesus' command for his followers to love and serve) one another, following his example. The two major symbolic activities of the evening are the washing of feet, as servants to one another, and the celebration of the Lord's Supper, remembering Christ in the manner he commanded his disciples.

APPLICATION

This service format can be used as an alternative observance for Holy/Maundy Thursday for ecumenical groups or a gathering without benefit of clergy. It involves a simple blessing of bread and the fruit of the vine.

Appropriate music may be played at the discretion of the community celebrating. The power of music is encouraged to augment the outline below and to serve as an accompaniment to the actions of those gathered.

SET UP

This ecumenical service works in various arrangements of space, depending on the location, numbers, etc. Care should be taken for how things are assembled and arranged for this service. It is a night for special beauty, meaning, and thoughtfulness. The following stations are used in the prayer and are fully preset before peoples' arrival:

1) Setting for the foot washing, including seats, basins, pitcher, water (warm and scented?), towels, all in sufficient number for the expected assembly.

2) A setting for the Lord's Supper, including bread and wine/juice in appropriate vessels, single or multiple cups.

3) A "garden" meditational area with plants, flowers, candles, arranged beautifully, with a feel for meditation.

There is a worship aid with the text for each person. All read the parts in bold. Music can be used in the background of each activity or an appropriate song may be sung to accompany the activity if the group is larger. A leader or several readers may be helpful, as would someone to help with the action at each of the stations. Appropriate icons or images may also be used in the context of each space.

If space and numbers allow, the service can be knit together by several processions (simple in silence, or formal with music) from one space to another, including a transitional space at the beginning.

CALL TO PRAYER

Can include an overview of Holy Thursday and the path of the liturgy/service. A general call to mindfulness is guided by a leader.

Dedicated with gratitude to Eileen O'Brien

CALL TO PRAYER

(leader or speaker)

GATHERING RITE

(This can take place in some outside space or in the table space. As the sun is setting, a leader comes into the space and addresses the congregation.)

Leader:
(in these or similar words):

The Lord Jesus is with us.

All: Now as always, the Lord is here among us.

My friends,
we are gathered here
    this evening to close
        our Lenten journey
and to begin the Triduum,
the great three-day liturgy
    of the Church that celebrates
        the life,
passion, death, and resurrection
    of our Lord and Savior,
        Jesus Christ.

As we make the journey
through these days of prayer
    and ceremony,
we remember what Christ
    has accomplished for us
        in his own life,
and we also recall the model
    on which our lives are built:
the service, sacrifice, and rebirth
    of Jesus of Nazareth.

This evening,
we will wash one another's feet
    as a sign of our willingness to
    follow the example given to
        us by Jesus the Servant;
we will share a feast recalling
    the ancient story of Exodus
and the journey of our ancestors
    in faith, the Jewish people;
and we will bless and break
    bread and share the fruit
        of the vine,
mindful of the Last Supper
    of Jesus and the gift to all
        who would follow him.
We will end our prayer
        "in the garden," spending
        time in solemn quiet
as we remember Jesus' struggle
    with his betrayal, his mission,
and the challenge of
    his own death.

As we prepare to remember
    again our great story,
let us bow our heads and pray.

(We keep a moment of silence.)

Let us pray together:

ALL: **Eternal God, lover
    of us all,
gather us now into
    Your Holy Spirit,
and be with us again
    as we prepare to enter
the mystery of
the passion, death,
    and resurrection
        of Your Son, Jesus.**

**Help us to relive
    the great story
        of our faith,
that we might better live
    the commandment
    given to us through
    Jesus, to remember him
    through service to others,
    self-sacrifice, and the
    breaking of the bread.**

**Make us open to the grace
    You extend to us
through the wonderful
    and terrible gift
        of the cross.**

**Through our prayer
    and fellowship
        this evening,
may we be strengthened
    for the journey
each of us must make
    in You.**

**We ask this through Christ,
    our Lord.**

Amen.

OPTIONAL PROCESSION AND/OR SONG

(If the service began in a transitional space, entrance with a simple or formal procession to the first station can be accompanied by a song as numbers permit.)

(Music option: "The Servant Song" [Gillard].)

(When at the place for foot washing:)

Leader: Let us be (seated and be) attentive to the word of God.

GOSPEL READING

John 13:1–15

(The following is read by a narrator [N] and two additional readers [R1 and R2], or assembly.)

N: A reading from the holy Gospel according to John.

Before the feast of Passover, Jesus realized that the hour had come for him to pass from this world to the Father. He had loved his own in this world and would show his love for them to the end.

The devil had already induced Judas, son of Simon Iscariot, to hand Jesus over. And so, during the supper, Jesus, fully aware that he had come from God and was going to God the Father who had handed everything over to him, rose from the meal and took off his cloak. He picked up a towel and tied it around himself. Then he poured water into a basin and began to wash his disciples' feet and dry them with the towel he had around him.

Thus he come to Simon Peter who said to him,

R1: "Lord, are you going to wash my feet?"

R2: "You may not realize now what I am doing, but later you will understand."

R1: "You shall never wash my feet!"

R2: "If I do not wash you, you will have no share in my heritage."

R1: "Lord, then not only my feet, but my hands and head as well!"

R2: "Those who have bathed have no need to wash, except for their feet. They are entirely cleansed, just as you are, though not all."

N: The reason Jesus had said, "not all are washed clean" was that he knew his betrayer. After he had washed their feet, he put his cloak back on and reclined at table once more. He said to them.

R2: "Do you understand what I just did for you? You address me as 'Teacher' and 'Lord,' and fittingly enough, for that is what I am. But if I washed your feet—I who am Teacher and Lord—then you must wash each other's feet.

What I just did was to give you an example: as I have done, so you must do."

N: Let those with ears to hear, now hear.

All: Thanks be to God.

(There is a moment of quiet following the gospel reading.)

THE FOOT WASHING

Leader:
In the life and times of Jesus,
hosts showed simple hospitality
    by washing the feet of guests
who came in from dusty roads.

We come to our paschal
    banquet this evening
from the dusty road

of our Lenten journey.
And, following the example
    of the Lord,
we bend to welcome in
    and to serve one another.

(A leader gives a few words encouraging the people to enter into the foot washing rite. There is a brief explanation of the procedure, its importance in the life of the Church, and its significance to the local community.

Following the exhortation, a leader or leaders get up and go to a foot-washing station. [As numbers dictate,] three or four people come to have their feet washed by the leader. They then go to the other stations where they proceed to wash the feet of the person who comes first to that station.

The first three or four people remain at the stations to assist others doing the foot washing [pour water, hand towels, assist people getting up and down, etc.], which happens in "relay style" [or in another format that better fits numbers, space, etc.].

Meditational music is played or an appropriate song is sung. The music comes to a close after all who wished to have their feet washed have done so.

(There is a brief moment of quiet.)

INVITATION TO THE FEAST

Leader *(In these or similar words:)*

In the story of Jesus
    and his last days,
we have this image of service
    to the servants
and a feast that was part
    of their Jewish history
that would become one
    of the core images
        of the Reign of God:
a table where all are welcomed,
a table where we become
    transformed.

Let us go now to our banquet,
a meal of hope and remembrance,
a sign of the love
    and presence of the Lord.

(Optional procession and/or song. If the foot-washing took place in another space, transition [with a simple or formal procession] to the next station can be accompanied by a song [e.g., Taizé's "Ubi Caritas] as numbers permit.)

THE PASCHAL FEAST

(This space is prepared as simply and as beautifully as possible with tables, tablecloths, candles, sufficient fresh bread for all, and fruit of the vine. This night the symbol of the shared cup is central. Options are played out according to the needs of the community. There is an option here for another leader to take over.)

WELCOME TO THE FEAST AND SIGN OF PEACE

Leader *(In these or similar words:)*

My friends,
we are a people bound in faith
    over many generations
to the Lord Jesus
through the breaking
    of the bread and the sharing
        of the cup.
In doing this tonight,
    we are especially connected to
the Healer/the Teacher
    who changed history
because of his faithfulness
    to the One who called him.

This evening we have already
    followed one of
        the mandates of this feast,
to wash one another's feet.
Now we remember Jesus
    in the manner that he
        put forth to us
before his betrayal
    and execution.

Before we settle in
    to bless our gifts,
let's share with one another
    the gift of peace.

(All share some sign of peace. Music may be played at this time.)

Welcome Holy Springtide

My friends,
everyone,
each of you, and any stranger
    waiting at our door
is truly welcome to this table
    with the welcome extended
        by Jesus.

Let us open our hearts to his
    presence and open our ears to
hear the story of this holy night.

GOSPEL READING

Matthew 26:17–30

(The following is read by a narrator [N] and two additional readers [R1 and R2], or assembly.)

N: A reading from the holy Gospel according to Matthew.

On the first day of the Festival of Unleavened Bread, the disciples came to Jesus and asked,

R1: "Where do you want us to make preparations for you to eat the Passover?"

N: He replied,

R2: "Go into the city to a certain man and tell him, 'The Teacher says: My appointed time is near. I am going to celebrate the Passover with my disciples at your house.'"

N: So the disciples did as Jesus had directed them and prepared the Passover.

When evening came, Jesus was reclining at the table with the Twelve. And while they were eating, he said,

R2: "Truly I tell you, one of you will betray me."

N: They were very sad and began to say to him one after the other,

R1: "Surely you don't mean me, Lord?"

N: Jesus replied,

R2: "The one who has dipped his hand into the bowl with me will betray me. The Son of Man will go just as it is written about him. But woe to that man who betrays the Son of Man! It would be better for him if he had not been born."

N: Then Judas, the one who would betray him, said,

R1: "Surely you don't mean me, Rabbi?"

N: Jesus answered,

R2: "You have said so."

N: While they were eating, Jesus took bread, and when he had given thanks, he broke it and gave it to his disciples, saying,

R2: "Take and eat; this is my body."

(In whatever manner suits the numbers and setting of the gathering, bread is lifted in blessing, broken, shared at table, and eaten by all. This is perhaps best accomplished in quiet. When all have eaten, the reading continues.)

N: Then he took a cup, and when he had given thanks, he gave it to them, saying,

R2: "Drink from it, all of you. This is my blood of the covenant, which is poured out for many for the forgiveness of sins. I tell you, I will not drink from this fruit of the vine from now on until that day when I drink it new with you in my Father's kingdom."

(In whatever manner suits the numbers and setting of the gathering, fruit of the vine is lifted in blessing, shared at table, and drunk by all. This is perhaps best accomplished in quiet. Then the reading continues.)

N: When they had sung a hymn, they went out to the Mount of Olives.

(Optional procession and/or song. If another space is available for the final station, transition there [with a simple or formal procession] can be accompanied by a song as numbers permit. If no additional space is available, candles from the table can be moved to the center of the room, room lighting may be shifted, an icon can be brought to the center, a reader may be placed in the center, or some other simple shift of scene can designate the next station.)

(Music option: "Jesus, Remember Me" [Taizé].)

(There is an option here for another leader to take over.)

AT THE GARDEN—PRAYER AND BETRAYAL

Leader *(in these or similar words:)*

My friends,
many parts of the story
    of Jesus are challenging.
The night in the garden before
    his betrayal is especially
    difficult to take in.
Let us open ourselves to hear
    the story of this painful night.

GOSPEL

Mark 14:27–50

(The following is read by a narrator [N] and two additional readers [R1 and R2], or assembly.)

N: A reading from the holy Gospel according to Mark.

Then Jesus said to them,

R1: "All of you will have your faith shaken, for it is written: 'I will strike the shepherd, and the sheep will be dispersed.'
But after I have been raised up, I shall go before you to Galilee."

N: Peter said to him,

R2: "Even though all should have their faith shaken, mine will not be."

N: Then Jesus said to him,

R1: "Amen, I say to you, this very night before the cock crows twice, you will deny me three times."

N: But Peter vehemently replied,

R2: "Even though I should have to die with you, I will not deny you."

N: And they all spoke similarly.

Then they came to a place named Gethsemane, and Jesus said to his disciples,

R1: "Sit here while I pray."

(Music option: "Stay With Me" [Taizé].)

N: He took with him Peter, James, and John, and began to be troubled and distressed. Then he said to them,

R1: "My soul is sorrowful even to death. Remain here and keep watch."

N: He advanced a little and fell to the ground and prayed that if it were possible the hour might pass by him; he said,

R1: "Abba, Father, all things are possible to you. Take this cup away from me, but not what I will but what you will."

N: When he returned he found them asleep. He said to Peter,

Welcome Holy Springtide

R1: "Simon, are you asleep? Could you not keep watch for one hour? Watch and pray that you may not undergo the test. The spirit is willing but the flesh is weak."

N: Withdrawing again, he prayed, saying the same thing. Then he returned once more and found them asleep, for they could not keep their eyes open and did not know what to answer him. He returned a third time and said to them,

R1: "Are you still sleeping and taking your rest? It is enough. The hour has come. Behold, the Son of Man is to be handed over to sinners. Get up, let us go. See, my betrayer is at hand."

N: Then, while he was still speaking, Judas, one of the Twelve, arrived, accompanied by a crowd with swords and clubs who had come from the chief priests, the scribes, and the elders. His betrayer had arranged a signal with them, saying, "The man I shall kiss is the one; arrest him and lead him away securely." He came and immediately went over to Jesus and said, "Rabbi." And he kissed him. At this they laid hands on him and arrested him.

One of the bystanders drew his sword, struck the high priest's servant, and cut off his ear. Jesus said to them in reply,

R1: "Have you come out as against a robber, with swords and clubs, to seize me? Day after day I was with you teaching in the temple area, yet you did not arrest me; but the scriptures must be fulfilled."

N: And they all left him and fled.

(Music option: a cappella "Were You There?")

(There is a period of silence, followed by silent closing and departure. There is also an option for a vigil of prayer into the night if a place is available for such.)

■ ■ ■

HOLY SATURDAY

Homecoming

Abba—
is this night?
Am I sleeping?

What kind of sleep is this?
It is so cold. This bed is hard.
There is no window.
I can't see the moon.
There was a beautiful
    spring moon.
Where is it now?
Where are the stars?

My arms, my legs,
all of me is cold as earth.

How did I come to be here?

I remember a dream:
a sad, heartrending dream.
I was so alone.
And I was calling to You,
and I was afraid You would
    not be with me.

I was something torn
    and ragged on a tree,
and the wind came
and swept me away
and brought me here
and quieted me.

Abba,
now I am dreaming of You.
And I think I can see
a little of the stars
and maybe the first touch
    of the sun.

Abba,
I think I can see Your face.
It is so beautiful to me,
just as I remember.

■ ■ ■

Easter Sunday Dawn

From the Scattered Brotherhood
DEDICATED TO MY BROTHER, RICHARD MICHAEL PHILLIPS

*"Early on the first day of the week,
while it was still dark…"*
(John 20:1a)

There were those of us who
took to the shore,
the wood, the edge
   of wilderland,
to wait for what we could
   not know.

However fearful of
   our separation from you,
to stay together
in that room choked with dread,
shadowed sweat,
   and incomprehension
was too much.

We understood the sequestered
   knot of those closest to you,
     gathered
in their own secret sadness,
but we scattered few
ached for grasses,
   familiar stones,
the lacey arcs of tree branches,
any place or thing that bore
association with you.

We had to go near
   those open spaces
where we knew you, heard you,
   where we tangled
with the seeming impossibilities
of your frequent clarity.
Places of bread, laughter, talk,
and transformation
that happened without our ever
   really being aware.

Then,
drifting to more private places
where, later, we each wrestled
with the conundrum of loss,
our minds shredded on the
   reality that, yes, you meant it,
about the dying.

We thought you wrong,
mistaken, misinterpreted.
Unaware of the light that
we saw in you, for sure, lasting.
Of course you would be with us,
long into our given days.
Our older ages would still bear
the mark of your words, touch,
and shining eyes.
And these things would keep us
young.

In that changeling, aching dark
before sunrise, we wandered
separate,
souls frayed, confounded but
   un-numbed, dazed with pain
cultivated in so brief
   a set of days
that weighed upon us like ages.

When, in our differing places,
the sky began to lighten,
we barely took notice,
thought it was the regular
   clockwork of the Earth,
the necessary and indifferent
   turning of the heavens
that could do nothing
to illuminate or warm any of
us, shrouded but walking about,
   incomprehensibly,
dead, but not.

Then, over water, a breeze,
warm, as a hand's touch upon
   the face, ripples the hard,
     dark glass of
the morning lake into a million
scales of gold.
Then, through tall grass and
   purple wildflower, a breath
presses down the blades
   and blooms,
     like footfalls,
       walking to each of us.

Then, in tree branches above,
   a sound,
for sure the reverberance
   of a quiet, known voice,
speaks wordlessly our names.

Then, a harsh trick of longing?
   the madness
     of remembrance?
     an illusion of pressing need?
but over everything,
a new light emerges—
and something in us
pushes against the stone burden
set upon our hearts,
and rises after all.

The sky is beribboned
   with unanticipated radiance,
and something in us knows.

We turn from our separate
   meanderings
toward one another,
sure that we will find you
There.

■ ■ ■

Easter Meditations

Although many treat Easter, like Christmas, as a one-day event, the Church invites us to consider the extraordinary event for a while—a long while. Fifty days in fact. Weeks and weeks to ponder this odd occurrence of rolled away stones, disillusioned friends trying to sort things out in the face of loss, reports of sightings and beachside chats with a man thought dead—individuals and communities are not likely to sort out what all that means for a long time.

I really like the formal, churchy name given to this period of trying to understand what has come to pass—*mystagogia*, a term especially applied to the newly baptized in the Church. (The process of conversion has been and still is one of the intents of the Lent/Easter season.) In one sense, it is a deliberate period of entering more deeply into the Mystery. In the Roman rites of Christian initiation, the process is done in community.

These meditations are part prayer and part imaginative engagements with others who have made that first Easter journey (including a reflection on Judas—I would not be the first to wonder how far the forgiveness of the cross might reach). I offer them with the hope that they will stimulate some of your own mystagogical contemplations.

Paschal Lesson

No matter
too-large crowds,
   steeped in lily's scent,
the profusion of trumpets,
incessant acclamations
   of ancient joy.
No matter
the gleam of colored
   and oiled eggs
glinting in strings
   of cellophane grass,
pastel shining of wrapping foils,
   unshook.
No matter.
It is an unlustrous Easter.

No columns of fire move me
   on my way.
No Passover bread sweetens
   my tongue.
No sprinkling of chilling water
   penetrates
this still-wintered hide.

Oh, yes, feet went washed.
Candles were lit.
Flames of first fire shed
   their dutiful light.
But the old stories
   rang hollow within
cavernous darks that
   would not yield.
The Sunday sunrise
   held no glint of
the miraculous.

Away from the bubbling
   crowds,
I bargain for a Lenten extension,
an "Incomplete"
to wear as protection
as I gather up excuses,
trying to be ready for
the One who'll come,
no doubt,
with gentle inquisitions and
waiting eyes.

Lacking Mary's vision,
I come to the garden to sit in
hard-held silence,
deaf to bird song,
blind to jonquil, hyacinth,
the heavy heads of tulips
bobbing agreeably
in a morning breeze.

A dull pupil,
I count the many stones,
unrolled,
wondering where,
so many Wednesdays ago,
I buried the Alleluia.
Was it stolen?
Snatched by dogs?
Pulverized by press of
earth?

How is it
ashes gave way not at all
   to transfiguring light,
to well-wet depths,
to cures,
to words like holy surgery?

How is it
hands,
smooth with so much that
   I did not do,
emerged uncrossed?

How is it
heart, still hard,
un-fleshed, unchanged,
gained nothing from a loss?

I cannot bear the answers,
or this mantle of
middle-age gray,
densely wound
about a child,
found dumb
at reckoning
on Easter day.

I stare at ground,
unbroken,
tough sod
   still stained November brown,
to find before me
   feet,
   bare, bruised,
   and cut with wounds
   round as lovers' rings,
new-flesh pink.

For all my wanting otherwise,
    my eyes stay down.
I wait,
    dreading the patience needed
      for lessons I never learn.

He sits beside me,
    fingering forsythia,
    trailing figures in sand,
    flat and freshly brushed.

His other hand,
    on my shoulders,
    bent as the arc
        of a spent moon,
He cradles my shame
    and my unknowing.

He sighs with me and whispers,
like a page of an opening book:
"In the Beginning…"
and, at last,
I find a bravery I do not own.
I turn
and look,
to see
    no face,
    but the trace of sun,
    piercing the willow,
    shimmering
    in the April wind.

■ ■ ■

Easter Gospel Meditation
Magdalene

"Early on the first day of the week, while it was still dark, Mary Magdalene went to the tomb…"
(John 20:1a)

I can still remember
   the morning:

There has never been such
   a darkness,
as if night would not relinquish
   my soul to day,
as if every shadow had made
   its home
in the hollow of my womb,
as if all my loss
had turned to stone,
and this stone
was rolled over the core of being.

It was the end of light.

I cannot remember
how I came to the garden.
I cannot recall
what moved my feet
to that place that was barren
despite the springtime,
because you,
my Beloved,
were no more.

I did not know
what I would find.
I remembered
your promise—
those words that infuriated
   so many,
     "In three days…"
I believed.

I could believe anything you said.

But I was also
there
for the insanity of the cross—

How many times
can a body be shattered?
How many ways
can flesh be shred?
How much wrong
can men wreak upon others
and call it justice?

I watched your mother,
wordless, beyond tears,
cradling you for a last time,
wiping those carpenter hands,
   limp, lifeless—
clearing fingers of grime,
blotting the last drops of blood.
Taking away that parody
   of a crown.
Searching your face
   for some trace of
the child that was still
   in the man.

We few women there,
only inches away,
could circle her
whose flesh encircled you,
our only embrace
in an hour bereft of kind touch.

Then
the dark, sour Sabbath:
bread that tasted not of joy
but of oblivion;
candles at sunset
that could not illuminate
   the room,
could not warm the chill
that held us in fierce suspension.

Then
the night:
terrible, sleepless wonder
that would not yield;
shards of dreams that repeated
only the horrors
of the street, the court, the hill.

Could hope
really die
in so brief a turn of days?
Could so great a love
lose its way
and vanish?

Dawn was no relief.
The first blushing of the sky
seemed wrong.
In the face of this loss,
night
should be forever.

Still,
in the quiet light
   I found my way to
that place
where I would make
   my last goodbye,
where words and sense would
   meet their utter end.

Ah, but for that parting,
who would roll away the stone?

Then
with the fire of the East
   behind your face
in a body free from death's cave,
in flesh strong,
unbruised,
new as the day—
   how could I know you?

I can taste the panic:

"Where have you taken him?"
To lose again what
   had been lost—
my brain was going to explode
and then
in the midst of acid madness
   setting in—
   my name.
You knew my name.
You knew me.
And suddenly
my unbirthed heart was
cradled in your voice.
And all of me ached to hold
   you,
to be held by you,
to erase the parade of loss.

   "Do not cling to me…"

I was stunned.
You were the watery depths
for whose baptism I longed,
and now
these words keep me away.
   But, Beloved,
   did you not see?
   My only thirst was for
you.

How I came
to the room
I am not certain.
Peter stared at me, breathless,
   incredulous,
shaking off the words I spoke.
His look said it:
"a woman in love, in grief—
that is all."
But he came to know
what I knew.
And they all came to know
what I know.

So now
at table again,
I taste you living in me still.
And before the closing
   of my day,
I breathe in again
the sweet wine of your voice
calling my name,
naming me
Beloved.

■ ■ ■

Welcome Holy Springtide

Easter Gospel Meditation

Peter

"When they had finished eating, Jesus said to Simon Peter, 'Simon, son of John, do you love me more than these?' 'Yes, Lord,' he said, 'you know that I love you.' Jesus said, 'Feed my lambs.'"
(John 21:15)

How often the others
    laughed at me.
I was so good at
    bungling things up.
I was always rushing so fast,
I had a hard time keeping
    my feet in line.
If there were a jar or a chair
    to trip over,
I was there.

I had a gift for certain kinds
    of calamity.
Even our fishing nets,
straight when we first left shore,
could be tangled in my hands
before we could even
    lay them out.

And he laughed too,
but it sounded different
    in my ears
than the laughter of James
    and John.
His laughter healed me
like the sound of the surf.

And when I blurted
    things out—
God! What a fool I could be!—
he'd just say:
    "Peter. My Rock."
And I felt less like a clod
for the sound of his voice.

On that horrid night,
when the mockery of a trial
was muffled in the court
    of the Sanhedrin,
every sound I heard
terrified me.
My name spoken
    on another's lips
could mean my death.
And his name
spoken on that night
could be the ruin of any man.

Keeping silent was
    my only protection.
It was cold in those hours
    before dawn.
I tried to get by the courtyard fire.
I couldn't go.
I found it hard to stay,
and that damned servant girl
kept taunting me.

I didn't know what I was saying
    at first;
fear just seemed to supply
    the words,
'til that blasted rooster
shattered the night
like an explosion in my head.

Then
I knew I was saying
what I promised
I wouldn't say.
And beneath the crowing
and my swearing that I didn't
    know him
came that voice:
    "Peter.
    My Rock."
And everything
caved in inside
with the rushing sound
of some dark, cold ocean stream.

If I hadn't heard his voice again,
I would have drowned forever.

...

Easter Gospel Meditation

The Centurion

"When the centurion and those with him who were guarding Jesus saw the earthquake and all that had happened, they were terrified, and exclaimed, 'Surely he was the Son of God!'" (Matthew 27:54)

They said
I would just get used to death:
   the shows of force,
   the torture, humiliations,
   ratty skin,
   protrusion of human guts,
   bodies oozing their last fluids,
   a feast for flies,
   the unnatural coloring
     of the dying
   and the corpses…

The stench of Golgotha,
   my commander told me,
was best erased with
   a good strong wine.

And they said,
you do enough of these
and your ears grow dead
   to the sounds of suffocation,
     and the cries of the always-
       innocent,
   to the taunts of those
   lucky enough not to be
   strung up
   on our trees of death,
and your heart hardens
   to the mothers clinging
   to the feet of their dying sons,
   wrenched into silence
   with the deepest agony.

It's enough that the bystanders
   are afraid,
they said.
   Stand by.
   Look fierce.
   Talk tough.
   That's your job, soldier;
   get good at it
   and the Empire
   might bring you home—
   to your family
   a little vineyard maybe,
   some brats at your feet,
     and inescapable
   memories.

That's what they told me.

And I guess,
I got good
at being
a little dead
myself.

Until that day
when the well-practiced
   killing routines
were no defense against
   what I saw in the heavens,
   what I heard from the cross,
   what I tasted in the air,
   what I felt all around me,
   when I saw his mother's face
     contorted and calm
       all at once,

when I heard him cry,
   just before death,
   not a curse,
   but forgiveness.

What kind of man was this?

And after that,
I just was no good
   for killing anymore.

They said
   I lost my touch.
They said
   it happens sometimes,
     even to the best.

And now,
they don't say much
   to me anymore at all,
because,
they say,
   this last one
   made me different.
   It made me a stranger.
And all I know
   as I look to the past
   with my shadow
   nailed
   at the foot of his cross—

This new stranger
   is a better man
   than the man
   I was before.

∎∎∎

Easter Gospel Meditation
Judas

"When morning came, all the chief priests and the elders of the people took counsel against Jesus to put him to death; and they bound him and led him away and delivered him to Pilate the governor. When Judas, his betrayer, saw that Jesus was condemned, he repented and brought back the thirty pieces of silver to the chief priests and the elders, saying, 'I have sinned in betraying innocent blood.'"
(Matthew 27:1–4)

Yes.
It is my darkest deed
and my bitterest word,
and you all judge me harshly,
   I know.

Mine is the great act
   that is never forgotten,
the horrifying utterance
   that is never retrieved,
the simple thing that slips
   out of your lips
     almost as if you mean it,
   but maybe
   you think
   you do not.

And it changes everything.

Oh, all you who sit
   in timeless shadows:
   Be careful of certainty.
   Be careful of believing
   the thing you do is the
   ONLY
   right thing.
   Be careful of the choice made
     in secret,
   and the decision forged
     past midnight
   when you think God sleeps.

You in the shadows:
   Can you know what it is
   when the thing you love
   and the thing you hate is all
   one?

Can you know what it is
   when dreams and hopes
   and reality
   collide?

Can you judge the soul
   hooked on its own
     fragile suppositions,
   tortured by a compulsion
     to act
   so rashly?

I only know,
   that when I looked into
     his face,
   I found
   no judgment there,
   only, still,
   love.

but, it seems, by then,
it could not change anything…

Yet, still,
in the stained fog
where I am bound
agelessly,
I see his face
and eyes that
alone
can bear to hold me.

■ ■ ■

Grace at a Springtime Meal

Leader (*lifting up spring blooms*):

Blessed are You,
Mysterious God, force
    beneath this spring time.
Through Your goodness
the impossible happens
    every year.
Earth surrenders what it can
    no longer hide,
and, faster than eye can catch,
flower,
tree,
shrub,
burst all bonds and bloom.

All: Thank You for the ways
    You renew us!

Leader (*lifting up fresh bread*):

Blessed are You,
Wondrous God,
    Maker of the Universe.
Through Your goodness
the earth brings forth food
to nourish,
to sustain,
to delight.

All: We thank You
    for what we
    share today
        with each other,
    and we ask Your grace
    to share what we have
    with those who
        have need.

    **Thank You for all
        the ways You feed us.**

(*We lift up the hands of those who dine beside us.*)

Leader:
Blessed are You,
Holy God, Maker of Humankind.
Through Your goodness
we are part of the human family.
We love.
We labor.
We grow together.

All: We thank You
    for who we are
    with each other,
    and we ask Your grace
    to share our gifts
        and talents
    with those who
        have need.

    **Thank You for all
        the ways You love us.**

Leader: May this springtime renew us in hope and strength.

All: May we be always
    mindful of Your
        gifts to us!

Amen.

■ ■ ■

Paschal Prayer and Meditation

Gracious God,
source of eternal love
    and possibility,
        Creator of us all—
in this Easter season,
for those with eyes to see,
everything is transformed
    and renewed
in the mystery of resurrection.

We ask on this day
for the power and the grace
to see Your Son
risen
in all those places
we have thought it impossible
for him to be:
    in our own hearts,
    still sluggish
    after less-than-successful Lents;

    in the shadowed places
    and the iffy places
        of human experience,
    where stones of every kind
    lay firm in their footings;

    in the rough places
    still waiting for
        an Advent smoothing
    that did not, could not come.

O Beloved,
wilder in mercy
    than we can fathom,
grant us a deeper taste
    of that Passover cup
wherein our senses
    may inebriate,
and our seeing
    may more fully blur
        at the edges,
till the deep Real be imaged—
in that same way that
caused Your Christ, raised high,
to spread arms eagle wide,
    and so embrace
all
the broken world
in blood and light.
Amen.

Reflections for Spring:

What do I notice around me?

What do I notice within me?

Where do I feel a stirring?

Where do I feel hope
    for the future, my future?

Where do I sense
    God's presence?

Where do I need the energy
    of God in this season?

■ ■ ■

A Table Prayer

For Good Shepherd Sunday

BACKGROUND

Before the cross was the ubiquitous symbol of Jesus in the Christian community, before the stern and bearded king, before the cosmic emperor enthroned, it was the beardless young shepherd painted on frescoed catacomb walls and sung about in church psalms who served as the image of the Lord. To encounter this young, pastoral image in the season of the resurrection is no accident. The Good Shepherd is a long-rooted image (Psalm 23) in Jewish prayer imagery. He factors in as a basic reality of life in societies less separated from agriculture. And his appearance in a post-Easter cycle of readings is a great comfort for a people that remembers the harsh pains of crucifixion and separation—and perhaps questions, "why?" The Shepherd has staying power; he abides, survives, and is passionate about retrieving the lost.

APPLICATION

Certainly this prayer works for a gathering on "Good Shepherd Sunday" in the Easter season. As with other table prayers in this collection, it works well for an alternative (priestless) Sabbath gathering, RCIA, parish meetings, family gatherings, retreats, ecumenical gathering of several communities, etc. This prayer form lends itself to a potluck. A student colleague of mine once introduced me to the concept of the Shepherd's Feast in Eastertide. A Mediterranean menu of olives, pita bread, goat cheese, dates, figs, etc. (which we ate on rugs on the floor) provided a backdrop for a conversation about what the resurrection meant to each of us.

SET UP

This is prayed by a group gathered around a single (expanded) table, or at a series of tables (or try the Shepherd's Feast outdoors or on rugs). Tables can be set as simply or as elaborately as resources allow. Images/icons of the Shepherd may be useful, and different small images may even be placed at each seat. Additional environment depends on community resources and creativity.

At the table, all have a copy of the text and a glass. The fruit of the vine (wine or juice) is distributed to each person's glass. A loaf of bread for breaking is in readiness at a leader's place, or a loaf can be present at each table.

This setting for a table prayer includes various spots for music. Resources of the community will dictate this, of course, but if musicians are not present, recorded music may assist. A cappella renderings of song should not be dismissed altogether, particularly if the feast happens out of doors.

Individuals read the numbered portions (this can be designated in advanced or done at table, spontaneously). All read the parts in bold.

CALL TO PRAYER

The meal begins with an indication of the nature of the prayer, some sort of call to mindfulness (quiet, intentional breathing or meditational music or song). A designated leader lights a candle and begins with the gospel reading when all are ready.

PRAYER

John 10:11–18

Do you know that the Lord is here?

> **The Lord is with us indeed.
> Alleluia.**

Are your hearts lifted up?

> **We are lifting them now
> to the One who
> shepherds us.**

Why are you here?

> **We are here to give thanks
> and praise
> to the One who has saved us.**

1) Gracious Lord,
in our immeasurable journey
 through time and space,
we have wandered both near
 to you and far from you.

> **And through the ages,
> in the voices of prophets,
> through the revelations
> of Your creation,
> and in the teachings
> of holy women and men,
> you have called to us
> as a shepherd that
>   summons the flock.**

2) We know you as teacher,
with words that call us over the centuries.

> **You show us a new way
> to the Father.
> You speak mystery
> and passion
> with words that challenge
> and inspire.**

3) We know you as healer,
bringing health and wholeness
 to body and soul.

> **You cleanse the leprosy
> of our minds.
> You mend the brokenness
> of our spirits
> and restore our hearts,
> impossibly, incredibly.**

4) And we know you as shepherd,
strong and able and ever young.

> **You summon us out
> of separation.
> You retrieve us from
> the dangerous places
> and gather us together.
> You abide.**

5) In our (evening) gathering,
in this blessed Eastertide,
we sing together with all those
who have been called
 throughout the ages,
saints and sinners alike,
the strong and the struggling,
the weak and the brave.

> **We lift our voices
> with all Creation
> to call back in love
> to the One who made us,
> formed us,
> and called us repeatedly
> to be wholly loved.**

Communal Song
(Options: "The King of Love My Shepherd Is," Psalm 100: "We are God's People" [Haas], "With Drums and Dancing" [Schutte].)

6) Holy One,
we are mindful in this season
 of spring
that the earth brings forth new life
in wonderful, wild,
 astounding ways.

> **We are mindful
> that grass and flower and tree
> all surge with energy.
> In garden, park,
> or sidewalk crack,
> that which was crushed
> and dead
> is regreening,
> is reborn,
> and we give thanks.**

7) Mighty One,
we are mindful in this season
 of rebirth,
that we are surrounded
 by new life—
creatures that are fabulous,
fragile, and miraculous.

> **We are mindful
> that bird and bug
> and furry beast
> are finding their space,**

their home,
in sky, under earth,
   in meadows.
**Eden enjoys a distant reprise,
   and we give thanks.**

8) Gracious One,
we are mindful in this season
   of Easter
that Your Shepherd Son
embraced every part
   of our humanity
and surrendered even to his
death.

**We are mindful
that love shattered
death's final door.
Mysteriously, wonderfully,
   beyond explanation,
we share in the legacy of the
children of God.
We too shall rise again,
   and we give thanks.**

9) And so, Most Loving One,
in that ancient simple way
with the fruits of first harvest,
with bread of gathered grains
and cup of crushed fruit,
we remember the life
   of Christ, our Shepherd,
and the life that we are called
   to share,

(We lift the bread in blessing.)

as together we pray:

**Bless this bread for our use,
Most High.
Let it be broken and shared,
sustenance for us all:
the lost, the outcast,
the sinner, the seeker.
For the gift of this,
for the blessing of this,
we give You thanks.**

(The bread is then broken and shared, and all eat.)

10) And again, Most High,
in the simple, sacred way,
we lift the cup of the fruit
   of the vine
toward our heaven-home
as we remember the gift
   of Christ, our Shepherd,
and the life that we are blessed
   to share,

(We lift the cup in blessing.)

as together we pray:

**Bless this wine for our use
Most High.
Poured out and shared,
delight and renewal for us all:
the longing, the tired,
the thirsty, the ready.
For the gift of this,
for the blessing of this,
we give You thanks.**

(The fruit of the vine is shared, and all drink.)

11) May our sharing
   of bread and cup
gather us more fully as your flock,
O Lord Jesus.

**May every table we share
be an open, welcome pasture
for all that long
   for your presence.**

12) May every broken loaf
be shared sustaining
   of your beloved ones,
O generous Lord Jesus.

**May every hunger
   that we know
find an answer
in the manifold ways
   that you feed us.**

13) May every shared cup
be vibrant, rich,
   and quenching mystery
for your wandering,
   waiting people,
O tender, strong,
   and steady Shepherd.

**May every thirst that we feel
find its answer
in the surprising ways
   that you
give us to drink.**

14) My brothers and sisters,
we have praised the Creator
who has brought us into being.
We have blessed the Lord
who has brought us together.
Let us thank the Spirit
who animates the presence
   of the Shepherd
for so many people,
over so many ages.

O Holy Spirit,
we thank You that You have
drawn us to this table,
to the feast of
   the Good Shepherd.
May his bread and cup
   strengthen us
and unite us as one flock
under one shepherd
   as he guides us
all our days:
in times of dark shadow,
and in time of bright
   abundance,
in seasons of dryness,
and in seasons
   of flowing waters
through this earthly passage,
even to the gates of heaven.

We pray together,
through the same Lord,
Jesus Christ.
AMEN.

CLOSING: SIGN OF PEACE AND/OR SONG

(Song options: "Lead Me Lord" [Becker], "Lead Me, Guide Me," "Just a Closer Walk With Thee.")

(Opportunity for potluck dinner or "Shepherd's Feast."

Possible Shepherd's Feast Menu:
- *Pita bread*
- *Goat or feta cheese*
- *Assorted olives*
- *Hummus*
- *Baba ganoush*
- *Stuffed grape leaves (dolma)*
- *Dried figs*
- *Dates*
- *Golden raisins*
- *Dried apricots*
- *Dried plums*
- *Wine/grape juice*
- *Mint tea)*

■ ■ ■

A Trinity Table Prayer

for Eastertide

APPLICATION

This works well throughout Eastertide for alternative (priestless) Sabbath gatherings, RCIA, parish meetings, family gatherings, retreats, an ecumenical gathering of several communities, etc. Trinity Sunday falls on the Sunday after Pentecost (at least in the Roman liturgical calendar) and this may prove useful in that specific context.

SET UP

This is prayed by a group gathered around a single table that can be set as simply or as elaborately as resources allow. Images/icons of the Trinity may be useful. The liturgical color for Easter and the Trinity is white, so white on white on white with candlelight could create a beautiful environment, depending on community resources and creativity.

At the table, all have a copy of the text and a glass. The fruit of the vine (wine or juice) is present at each table along with a loaf of bread. At the instruction of the leader, glasses are filled and an initial fragmentation of the bread takes place for each person.

This table prayer can be kept simply as is, or it could include various spots for music. Resources of the community will dictate this, of course, but if musicians are not present, recorded music may assist. A cappella renderings of song should not be dismissed altogether, particularly if the songs chosen are well-known hymnody.

Individuals read the numbered portions (this can be designated in advanced or done at table, spontaneously). All read the parts in bold.

CALL TO PRAYER

The meal begins with an indication of the nature of the prayer, some sort of call to mindfulness (quiet, intentional breathing or the ringing of a chime or meditational music, etc.). A designated leader lights a candle and, perhaps, lights some form of incense to underscore the miraculous and mysterious nature of the theme. The leader instructs the fragmenting of bread and the pouring of the fruit of the vine.

CALL TO PRAYER

(*As described. We begin by first breaking and taking the bread, and by pouring out a cup of the fruit of the vine for each person. When all are ready, we begin.*)

1) O God of Mystery,
in this new springtime
   of our life,

We bless You.

2) Source of all that is,
the Earth is being reborn again,

And we bless You.

3) Lover of us all,
in tree and flower,
in nest and burrow,
in river and farm field,
life is moving anew,

And we bless You.

4) Despite our bruising
   of her lands
and the poisoning of her waters,
even though we take her
   for granted
and ignore her many signs,
Your creation, our planet home,
sustains us still.

And so we bless You!

(*We lift up our hands and say:*)

**With new fire
   and ancient word,**

Welcome Holy Springtide

**with the gifts of the earth—
    our fragile bodies
        and eternal souls,
with all we are
    and may yet be,
we bless You, Holy God,
    our maker and sustainer.**

(We lower our hands and continue.)

(Option for music, verse of song: "God Is One, Unique and Holy" [Wren].)

---

5) O Beloved Shepherd,
in the company of your
    good people,

We bless You.

---

6) Our Saving Lord,
in this season of the Church's joy,

We bless You.

---

7) Jesus Our brother,
    teacher, Lord,
present to us in holy word,
present to us in loving Spirit,
present to us in enduring hope,
present to us who see you not,

We bless You.

---

8) Despite the many ways
    we crucify You
and entomb You still in silence,
even though we take You
    for granted
and resist Your call to us
    in Your little ones,
You, our teacher, risen lover, Lord,
reach out to us still.

And so we bless You.

(We each lift up our bread and say:)

**With new hope
    and ancient faith,
with the gifts of the earth—
    our holy bread
        from precious grain,
with all we know
    and may yet know,
we bless You, Jesus,
    Anointed One,
our liberator
    and companion.**

(We each eat of the bread.)

(Option for music, verse of song: "God Is One, Unique and Holy" [Wren].)

---

9) O Divine Presence,
drawn by Your grace,

We bless You.

---

10) Most Holy Wisdom,
in Your tender embrace,

We bless You.

---

11) Holy Spirit of God,
in inspired speech and song,
in acts of courage and love,
in compassion and justice,
in change and unfolding truth,

We bless You.

---

12) Despite the many ways
    we ignore You
and hide the gifts You give us,
even though we take You
    for granted
and close our hearts, ears,
    and minds,
You, passionate fire of God,
animate us still.

And so we bless You.

(We each lift up our cups and say:)

**With new prayers
    and ancient songs,
with the gifts of the earth—
    our blessing cup with
        the fruit of the vine,
with all we love,
    and may yet love,
we bless You, Great Spirit,
    our life-giver and renewer.**

(We each drink of the cup.)

(Option for music, verse of song: "God Is One, Unique and Holy" [Wren].)

**Blessed are You,
Triune and Holy God
    of the Universe,
in Your love You give us
bread and wine to nourish us
on the journey
    we make together.
May we know You present
    at all our tables,
and bless You and praise
    You all our days.**

AMEN.

■ ■ ■

The Easter Women

An Eastertide Service of Lessons and Carols

APPLICATION

The lessons and carols format is well-known in many churches at Advent or Christmastide. It is a service-form largely associated with the Anglican Church, having been inaugurated by a bishop in the late 1880s. Traditionally, a sequence of Old and New Testament readings, generally nine in number, tell the story of salvation interspersed by related hymns. The form is wonderful, reflective, and inspiring, and it allows for the visiting of new or beloved standard pieces of music. For this reason, other feasts of the year benefit from the format as well. The rendering below uses imaginative writings that extrapolate from lines of Scripture. It may be especially useful on a woman's retreat but does not require a single gender audience.

SET UP

This particular service can be prayed in a variety of locations, with inventive, interpretive use of space, depending on local talent and resources. The readings can be used in a setting without music. They could be interpreted by dancers/creative movement and combined with art work. If music is used, the space should be conducive to that art form.

The prayers in bold at the end of the monologues are meant to be congregational, so some sort of worship aid (paper or projected) is required.

Readers should be able to interpret the text very personally. (Please: rehearse and know the text.). There ought be some level of internalizing of the moods, shifts, and personalities. Pauses may be as significant as speech.

A reflection based on the women of Scripture can be woven throughout the readings, or delivered at one moment within the service. Sung or instrumental music can also act as an interlude or response between readings.

CALL TO PRAYER

(The service begins with an indication of the nature of the prayer, some sort of call to mindfulness [quiet, intentional breathing or the ringing of a chime or meditational music, etc.]. The theme of the readings is paschal transformation. We might start [or end] with reflection time about how we are transformed by the paschal mystery.)

1) MARY, THE MOTHER OF JESUS

Scripture Speaks
John 19:25–30

Mary Speaks
Reader: I always knew that he was destined for the edge of things.

He was constantly wandering out of my grasp as a child. He could wind up anywhere and feel at home amidst strangers. So many times I thought we'd lost him forever, but our searches would eventually lead to him, engaged with the oddest people, as if he belonged to them and we were but visitors.

Later, he would leave us for days at a time and go who knows where—the hills, the sea, just away. "What do you do there?" I would ask and, quietly, he would only tell me, "I listen."

Welcome Holy Springtide

And I felt I could ask no more.

In the later years, after the desert, when he was so changed, he would follow the voice that ruled his heart, and the voice led him where there was human hunger of the deepest kind. Rich, poor, clean, unclean, believers, outsiders—he didn't care. He was drawn by their need and by his own call. I could not stop him. I learned not to want to stop him—even when he walked into those places where anger roamed after him, like so many crazy dogs…There are times when you know that something just has to be, and you can only watch it happen.

So, that day on the hill, with the horrible crowds and so much pain, and—even for a Roman event—so much blood, I couldn't reach out to pull him back, no matter that every part of my body that had held him was straining to be around him again. He had slipped away, so far away, beyond my call and beyond any search. I went home with John and found that I was beyond tears myself. Everything had been ripped out of me.

But despite all that, despite the finality of the stone and the insult of the guard at his tomb, despite the lid of that night closing on everything, I prayed that he would find me this time, this hollowed-out vessel aching for some kind of filling.

And in a way that defies language and understanding, he did return to me again, so deeply to the center that I know he will always be with me, and no journey of his will remove him from me.

(There is a moment of silent reflection.)

ALL: **O Saving God, when all that truly matters to us has been taken from us, come to us in our emptiness and fill us anew with Your presence. Restore us to hope, even in the face of violence, death, and the world's discord. Let us know You are near to us in the hour of loss. AMEN.**

MEDITATION/ RESPONSORIAL SONG
("Mary, Did You Know?" or "Lift Your Voice, Rejoicing Mary")

2) THE WOMEN WHO ACCOMPANIED JESUS

Scripture Speaks
Mark 15:40–41

The Women Speak
(One or several readers.)
We are the mothers and the aunts and the confidantes.
We are the midwives and the shepherds of grief.

The swaddling clothes, the bridal veils, the table linens, and the funeral shrouds are all in our keeping.

With our linen strips, sweet oils, and tears, we go forward in the dance of loss.

The men we love tremble, hiding for good reason, knowing what a threat ideas and words can be, how laws and structures can entomb a vision, what monsters a dream will bring out of hiding, what strangling force waits in guarded buildings and the halls of power.

But we do the brave, quiet work of the ancient mothers. We wash away what we can of death, anoint what we may of battered flesh, and lay down our hope on stone as gently as we would a sleeping baby, wondering when it will wake again.

And until it wakes, we hold a space for it within us. It is what we do. It is what we know.

(There is a moment of silent reflection.)

ALL: **O Tender God, give us the courage to be where grace and gift and compassion call**

us, especially when the powers of this world would have us gone. Help us to minister to those most in need, to the brutalized and the outcast, to the fragile face of God all around us. **AMEN.**

MEDITATION/RESPONSORIAL SONG *("Coventry Carol" or "Go, Bury Thy Sorrow" or "Sometimes I Feel Like A Motherless Child.")*

3) THE WIFE OF PILATE

Scripture Speaks
Matthew 27:17–19

Pilate's Wife Speaks
READER: He had come to listen little to me over the years.

Early on, he prized me: elegant, educated, intuitive, and moneyed—Claudia Procula. I was sufficient to bring him to Rome's attention. But when he became governor of that wretched place, he grew more and more removed from me. The fractious politics of occupied land troubled him, despite his stoic exterior. And those Hebrew mystics had a way of unsettling even him.

The morning of the trial was a normal one for him, but I was unsettled with a night of rare dreaming. I cannot recall the look of that dream, only how it sounded—screams and weeping, and the percussive rattle of Hebrew tongues chanting the Nazorean's name.

I was certain my husband would find it annoying, but the dream compelled my sending him the scroll with the words I suspected he would ignore. He was already in the thick of the web of things. There was small need for the slave to tell me he had no reply to give me; I knew the course of things by the shouting of the crowds.

And now rumors of this Galilean teacher's "resurrection" find us, even after these many years. Pilate laughs at the bizarre bits of news from Judea, but the laughter is forced for him, and it is his sleep that is broken, so frequently, with dreamed voices and, I think, a face. He wakes, trembling, and allows me to hold him like before.

I never dreamed that this crucified prophet would be the one to bring my husband back to me, to reach beyond my terrible dreams and restore some untouched part of my soul.

(There is a moment of silent reflection.)

ALL: O powerful God, reach to us out of time and place and touch us. Restore what has died in us. Stir up in us a new dream, a new vision, and bring us to birth as surely as the earth in spring. AMEN.

MEDITATION/RESPONSORIAL SONG *("The Dream of Pilate's Wife" [Baird].)*

4) THE BREAD WOMAN

Scripture Speaks
Mark 14:12–26

The Woman Speaks
READER: I had never poured my soul into a feast like this one. Imagine! *He* was coming to our house!

I had only heard about him. He had healed my sister and that caused her husband to stop drinking, and there were people in the neighborhood who had been there at the hillside when so many were so impossibly fed!

But this night he was coming to our house, and I was cooking for him. I would finally be at table with him. And he would be eating my good food.

I have never cooked a better Passover meal. The lamb was young, the garlic was fresh, and the herbs so supple and green— full of springtime. And the bread! Unleavened, but not without flavor!

I have never worked harder preparing a room. Everything was clean and pure. I brought out our best cloths. The lamps had new oil and new wicks. They would burn clean tonight.

Everything was ready when he came. But it turned into such a different meal than I had anticipated.

First, there was some oddness about foot-washing. He told our servants to be seated and he washed the feet of all our guests and of our servants too!

Then there was that troubling talk of betrayal. Someone left, I didn't see who it was. Everyone looked sad for awhile. But then, when it was time to bless the bread, I thought he would perhaps praise my baking. But instead he tore the bread so tenderly and gave it to us all;

"My Body," he said. And we ate what he gave to us stunned into silence.

What had he done to my bread?

And at the end, after the perfect lamb and the beautiful greens and the singing and the story and too much wine, he blessed one more cup, "My Blood," he said.

And we passed the cup and tasted sweetness and bitterness all at once, and I wondered what was happening to him, to us, to me.

They left a little while after. I couldn't blame them. It was perfect night to be out, so full of peace.

But I wanted to stay.

I sent the servants away; it was late. I stared at the platters. I sipped the last of the wine. I gathered all the crumbs. What had he done?

It seems I had never been so hungry and not known it.

It seems I have never eaten so little and found myself fed so well.

What had he done?

And now, in these days after his horrible death and the stories of his resurrection, bread is never the same anymore. And each meal feels different. We cannot forget him and because of that, every table top seems to bask in the glow of his presence. I can't explain it. I know my cooking hasn't changed, really, but it isn't ever just a meal anymore…

(There is a moment of silent reflection and an option for the communal sharing of bread.)

MEDITATION/RESPONSORIAL SONG
("Taste And See" [Haugen or Moore].)

5) MARY MAGDALENE

Scripture Speaks
John 20:11–18

The Woman Speaks
READER: I can still remember the morning. There has never been such a darkness, as if night would not relinquish my soul to day, as if every shadow had made its home in the hollow of my womb, as if all my loss had turned to stone and this stone was rolled over the core of being.

It was the end of light.

I cannot remember how I came to the garden. I cannot recall what moved my feet to that place that was barren despite the springtime because you, my Beloved, were no more. I did not know what I would find. I remembered your promise—those words that infuriated so many: "In three days…" I believed. I could believe anything you said. But I was also there for the insanity of the cross—how many times can a body be shattered? How many ways can flesh be shred? How much wrong can men wreak upon others and call it justice?

I watched your mother, wordless, beyond tears; cradling you for a last time; wiping those carpenter hands, limp, lifeless; clearing fingers of grime;

blotting the last drops of blood. Taking away that parody of a crown. Searching your face for some trace of the child that was still in the man.

But we few women there, only inches away, circled her whose flesh encircled you.

Then the dark, sour Sabbath: bread that tasted not of joy but of oblivion, candles at sunset that could not illuminate the room or warm the chill that held us in fierce suspension.

Then the night: terrible, sleepless wonder that would not yield, shards of dreams that repeated only the horrors of the street, the court, the hill…Could hope really die in so brief a turn of days? Could so great a love lose its way and vanish?

Dawn was no relief. The first blushing of the sky seemed wrong; in the face of this loss, night should be forever.

Still, in the quiet light I found my way to that place where I would make my last goodbye, where words and sense would meet their utter end. Ah, but for that parting, who would roll away the stone?

Then, with the fire of the east behind your face, in a body free from death's cave, in flesh strong, unbruised, new as the day—how could I know you?

I can taste the panic: "Where have you taken him?" To lose again what had been lost—my brain was going to explode; and then in the midst of acid madness setting in—my name. You knew my name. You knew me. And suddenly my unbirthed heart was cradled in your voice, and all of me ached to hold you, to be held by you, to erase the parade of loss.

"Do not cling to me…" I was stunned. You were the watery depths for whose baptism I longed and now these words keep me away. But Beloved, did you not see? My only thirst was for you?

How I came to the room I am not certain. Peter stared at me, breathless, incredulous, shaking off the words I spoke. His look said it: "A woman in love, in grief—that is all." But he came to know what I know. And they all came to know what I know.

So now at every table again I taste you living in me still. And before the closing of my day I breathe in again the sweet wine of your voice calling my name, naming me beloved.

(There is a moment of silent reflection—an option for the communal sharing of bread.)

(Optional reflection.)

Meditation/Responsorial Song
("Hymn for the Feast of St. Mary Magdala" [St. Helena Breviary], "Mary, First One to the Tomb" [Newton], "In the Garden" [traditional].)

FINAL PRAYER

ALL: **O Merciful Christ, like Mary of Magdala, Your faithful disciple, open our ears to the sound of Your voice. Help us to hear our name, the name of your beloved, resounding around us and within us. Help us to recognize and trust in Your presence, closer to us than we can name or know.**

May the power of Your resurrection be manifest in our words and works, that we may be a source of new life and new hope in our battered and crucified world.

Amen.

CLOSING SONG

("Easter Alleluia" [Haugen], "Up From The Earth" [Cooney], or "Darkness Is Gone" [Bell].)

■ ■ ■

Earth Day

In addition to the religious practices of Easter in spring, people across the world engage in many observances of Earth Day (generally April 22, though sometimes observed in March at the equinox). Born out of the landmark writing of Rachel Carson's 1962 bestseller *Silent Spring* and the protest culture of the 1970s, Earth Day has grown over the decades as concerns about environment have intensified and the reality of our sins against Creation have become painfully manifest. The day inspires political, social, economic, educational, and religious activity as we grow in awareness of the finite nature of the planet and its resources and of the interconnectedness of peoples and biosystems.

Although not specifically a "religious" event, Earth Day draws our prayerful concerns to the most basic "sacramental" thing—the Creation. It is no longer a function of science fiction, a notion of alarmist thinking, or "hippie new-agism" to care vibrantly about the planet, its creatures, and its natural systems. Nor is it an elective "secular" activity that does not necessarily invite the engagement of the people of God. We have left the "fill the earth and subdue it" phase of our religious development. Of necessity, we must be about the "right stewardship" of the Earth that we so definitely and drastically affect. It is one of the crosses that we must needs "take up" and do so with urgency.

Throughout the Christian world, theological stances that may have held a "God's going to take care of it all" point of view have changed to a greater acceptance of an environmental theology that recognizes a different relationship of humans to the world of which they are part. The growing awareness of the connection of all the components of the Earth also brings new dimensions to the understanding of the "body of Christ." Where one part of the body suffers, all really do suffer. And it also appears that the environmental disasters of our age are as compelling as any prophet's utterances. Thus, to live more consciously in the world, mindful of the impact of one's environmental choices, has become as much a part of spiritual practice as the very practical and concrete "Corporal Works of Mercy."

Since prayer and ritual can help alter our consciousness and our choices, the following pieces are offered. They are words of meditation, exultation, reverie, prayer, and penitence.

Earth Psalm

I love this planet home:
mountain rocks, rivers of dirt,
wild tree jungles full of more
    than I can name.
Spaces where we are
    and where we are not.

    I love her skies,
blue, plum-black,
    cloud-crowded,
changing, moving to a tune
    not made by me,
full of light and lights
    and untrammeled space.

    I love her big seas,
small lakes, shimmering ponds,
waters—rushing at midday,
still under moonlight,
themselves a home to
creatures vast, shining,
    mysterious.

I love the irrepressible growth of
green and brown and all colors
    sprung into flower shapes,
moss hidden in the dense,
moist roots of ancient elms
    or oaks or
other sacred limbs and trunks
and heaven-high leaves.

Monkeys, dogs, birds,
lions, lizards, gazelles,
great beasts and even serpents
(at a distance).
Creatures that escape
    our naming,
I love you, I am in awe of you,
and I pray for you,
that you may escape
even more of our rough touch
and consuming ways.

Oh, Earth, too wonderful
    to realize,
I bless you and all
    that made you.
Be strong enough to survive our
cancerous less-than-love of you,
and last,
despite us,
past our memory,
and be home, beloved,
to a brood better than ourselves.

◾ ◾ ◾

Welcome Holy Springtide

Another Creation Story

In Praise of Difference

> **APPLICATION**
>
> This Creation story emphasizes the differences inherent in the whole of the natural world. Variation is an inherent gift of all that is. This reading can be used for personal meditation or can be scored for a number of readers (solo voices with a larger verse choir). It is especially visual and imaginative, so it can be accompanied by art works (actually present or presented via PowerPoint slides). It could be accompanied by dance, creative movement, pantomime, masks, or puppetry. It's great for school groups where there are many potential players.

There are many stories of God
in many tongues,
    from many ages,
of how everything began,
of how earth and creatures
    came to be,
of how God came
    to be known—
stories of dark and light and
    mystery,
ends and beginnings.

This is another story:

Long ago,
longer than we have words for,
God was at play—
    giving birth to the universe,
spilling out children of God
from the body of God
and giving them a home
in the river of God that flowed
everywhere:
nebulae and gasses,
gatherings and explosions,
dark holes, brilliant stars,
whirling galaxies of colors for
    which we have no names,
planets with hearts
    of ice and fire,
creatures on planets that
    breathed night,
creatures that swam in the
    molten gold of suns…

God had big hands.
God had big ideas.
God found room for everything.
And God was delighted in this
    great goodness.

And because everything
    that God made
emanated music
dear to the ear of the Creator,
there was no end
to what God would make.

God loved the unending
    great song
that was happening,
with its many parts
    and sounds.

A big music that we cannot
    even name
but maybe could imagine,
if we could imagine
God imagining.

One day,
God looked
from the unrolling edge
    of everything,
amazed
at how different
    everything could be
and still be together.

God said,
"This difference is good.
There's so much now.
There's so much more
    that could be.

And no matter how much
   difference,
it is all a part of me."

Then God noticed
a small part of
The Great Everything
that seemed lonely.

So in that small corner
   of God's-Song-Unrolling,
God blinked a star
and whispered some planets
that made that star
their home.

And on one of those planets,
the Creator did in small
what had been done in big
throughout the whole
   of all God's work:

God made in miniature
what God had done everywhere:
   a gem of a place,
rough with rocks,
shining with waters,
shifting skies;
countless growing things,
green,
fuchsia,
brown,
vermilion,
flesh things,
fur things,
blue-feathered things carrying
   their song to the sun,
beasts bellowing daybreak at
   mountain edges,

silver creatures silently splitting
   dark ocean depths,
enameled bugs hiding in the red
   throats of orchids,
things invisible floating in the
   ether.

All different things
   with a wild music
that together
was God singing back to God.

And God said,
"All this everything,
all this difference,
listen how it sings together.
This is good."

Then God
tenderly bent down in the mud
and made creatures
so like God's self
that even God was amazed.

And God sighed.
And God's breath
slipped into human lungs,
and human flesh
entered into the song of
All Things Different
   and Together.

God and mud
And the countless voices of
   Earth were singing together.
For days and nights and days…

And it was good.

After a long while,
because God was so very big,
God said
to these creatures
   so much like God's self,

"I need to step a little away
and give you room to grow."

And the creatures born out
   of the mud cried out,
"Oh, but we are so much
   a part of you!
We will perish for want of
Your face,
Your voice,
Your touch,
Your song."

And God said,

"I have given you eyes,
 and ears, and touch,
   and taste, and more.
You will know me
   all around you:
in the groaning earth,
   in all her birthing,
in her high rocks
   and deep waters,
in the snow blast,
   in fog and rain.

"You will know Me
in the dance of the sun
   and turn of seasons,
in the creatures of flesh,
   fur, fin, feather,

Welcome Holy Springtide

in the secret things
    you cannot yet see
or have yet to name,
in the way that
all the different things of earth
move
and grow
and sing together.

"Do not worry.
I am in the Everything
    all around you."

And
so that they would remember
the unimaginable beauty
of God's face,
God made
the creatures of mud and spirit
brown and yellow
and white and black
and pink and beige
with eyes that glowed
like all the different kinds
    of stars that were
      shining
that very day,
all over the universe.

And,
so that they would remember
the great music
of the One Who Made Us,
God placed in the
multicolor creatures
    of mud and fire

so many sounds,
so many names for God,
so many languages for love,
so many dances to move
    to the music of God,
so many different ways for the
    music to be made,

that we,
the creatures of mud
and God's own breath,
should never forget
who we were,
who we came from,
and how every part of us
and our not-so-lonely planet
were different parts
of the great song of God.

■ ■ ■

Ascension Day Meditation
But Some Doubted

"Then the eleven disciples went to Galilee, to the mountain where Jesus had told them to go. When they saw him, they worshiped him; but some doubted. Then Jesus came to them and said, 'All authority in heaven and on earth has been given to me. Therefore, go and make disciples of all nations, baptizing them in the name of the Father, and of the Son, and of the Holy Spirit, teaching them to obey everything I have commanded you. And surely I am with you always, to the very end of the age.'"
(Matthew 28:16–20)

It's one of those lines
that I don't remember
having heard before.

Did someone slip that in
just for me?
    A faint lifeline thrown
    from down the ages,
    cast upon the seas of
    believing
    where, often enough,
    I flail fitfully?
A reminder that
    I am in notable company
    with the close-by eyewitness
    walk-and-talk-and-hear-him
    disciples?
As if to say:
    yes—
    this is more fabulous
    than mind can take in; You
    are not alone in incredulity.

We
are among those who fail
faith fullness.

"But some doubted."

For me this floats
    savingly
over waves of centuries,
a scriptural reprieve—
spelled out in three words.
For in these,
    my more latter days,
doubt has become
    that creaking creature
    with constant comment,
    somehow always
    at my elbow.
He critiques everything
(unbidden)
and no sacred thing
is spared his scrutiny.

So
as I strain to see my self
    standing
in the company of believers,
    staring
up towards Bethany's skies,
    seeking
to discern a perforated,
calloused foot
    dissolving
amidst an onrush of cloud,
he stands with me
and recounts:
    how sight fails,
    how gravity holds
    all things
    earth bound,
    how
    every
    human
    thing
    ends…

And then
four words:
    "I am with you…"
rise,
less obscure,
to calm the needlings
of chattering doubt.

And then
one:
    "always."
And I turn to see the faces
    of those who doubt as I do,
    of those affirmed in faith,
    of those who struggle,
    of those who fall
    discouraged,
    of those who rise again
    serene, if scarred,
    in the art of belief;
and in those faces,
    that Face emerges,
and even Doubt
must still his wounding words
for a moment as I dissolve
    out of singleness,
    out of separation,
into something greater
that endures
    "even to the very end."

■ ■ ■

Part III

The Long Arc of the Spirit: Summer Feasts

Memorial Day

A Remembrance

DEDICATED TO MY FATHER, GEORGE H. PHILLIPS

In a ritual I've never done,
   my father and I
      (my father's son)
took geraniums to
   the new-mown grave
     of his father
        and his father's bride.

The wide ride through
   a town too small took us
from market to graveyard,
   winding through streets
     of a history
I do not easily recall.
   Then, through iron gates,
to acres of hilly lawns
   with bad roads, too narrow,
crammed with dozens of cars
   in sentinel colors.

We rode in conversation
   with frequent, wide,
     and well-paved pauses.
We rode trying to trace
   the paths of a hidden history.

Against close-cropped green
   and the flecked grey stone,
deeper green leathery leaves
   stood flat and firm,
their rose-pink blossoms
   steamed a little,
their pungent herbal scent
   pressed out in
     the late May sun.

Amidst the yellow whine
   of lawn mowers and
the quiet ministrations
   of families at other graves,
we stood in an unplanned
   silence, feigning prayer,
closing eyes, blocking out
   the image of a stone
that bears his name,
with a set of years spanning
   three quarters of a century and
how many more?

Ready to leave before I had
   remembered much,
     or enough,
he uttered his inconclusive
   "Well..." and we resumed
our journey to not-quite-home.

I was pleased that he had taken
   me, somehow honored that
we had stood, however briefly,
   together,
before his father's name and our
   own not-so-distant deaths,
as if to say that if, over the span
   of not-shared years,
our lives had found too little a
   common ground, that now,
this plot of green, with its names
   and blooms and glassy stone,
might be one place where our
   differences dropped,
and a silent prayer made us,
   for a moment, one.

■ ■ ■

Ephphatha!

A Pentecost Invocation

BACKGROUND

Pentecost is a word from the ancient Greek that translates as "the fiftieth day." It is the Greek name for a significant feast in the calendar of ancient Israel that celebrates the giving of the Law on Sinai. This feast is still celebrated in Judaism as Shavuot. As the Christian liturgical year developed, Pentecost became a festival that observed the coming of the Paraclete, the promised Spirit, upon the early followers of Jesus. Fifty days after Easter, the Church celebrates its "birthday" with the wondrous outpouring of spiritual gifts that animated the followers of Jesus and strengthened and emboldened them to move out into the known world with good news. Its very nature invites energy, joyful liturgical expression, and perhaps a little more noise than we are used to.

APPLICATION

Veni Sancte Spiritus, Come Holy Spirit, is the cry of the day. It is the utterance of a people who are tired of being afraid, weary of their own complacence, thirsty for an outpouring of renewing energy, ready for the warming of life's flame within individuals and communities. This invocation can precede any number of events, meetings, feasts, liturgies. It can be combined with song. (One of my favorites chants is the African *Wa Wa Wa Emimimo*, which is plaintive and hypnotic in its repetition. The Taizé community also offers a number of lovely, soulful options.) Change the pronoun, and it is a good invocation for personal prayer as well. The prayer can be orchestrated for several voices or a whole congregation. Prayed earnestly, the invocation deserves to erupt into song at the end.

CALL TO PRAYER

The selection from the Gospel of Mark is not a typical Pentecost reading, but it feels wonderfully apropos for this invocation. It can be used as a call to prayer. If fitting, an explanation of the feast can be a part of the preamble to this piece. A community can call to mind ways that it may have blocked the animation of the Spirit; thoughtful silence may help clear the interior stage for possibilities of a freely invited Spirit.

READING AND INVOCATION

(A reader reads Mark 7:33–35.)

Come Irresistible Spirit!
Open us up!
Unstop our ears, our tongues,
our burdened hearts,
    our sluggish brains.
Let Your breath flow in spaces
    within us that we have closed
on purpose, by accident,
    without our knowing.
Open us! We are calling to You.

Come Most Holy Spirit!
Let us be opened
to a beginning,
    a host of possibilities,
a dream of becoming something
    not ever considered.

Come Gracious Spirit!
Let us be opened
to the sound of our name
    spoken in a new way,
    to an invitation we thought
    was meant for another but
    really is for us.

Come Singing Spirit!
Let us be opened
to voices that call for the gifts
    that only we can bring,
to ways of living that make sense
    more to the heart than
        to the wallet.

Come Wisdom Spirit!
Let us be opened
to who we are in truth,
to who we might become,
to what we can be on our own,
to what we might be together.

Come Powerful Spirit!
Let us be opened
to becoming more and more
a community that can change
the world.

O Holy Well of Grace,
both Fluid and Fire,
surround, indwell,
inspire, renew,
and let us,
for love's sake,
let us be opened!

(*Optional music.*)

■ ■ ■

Prayers of the People

For a Pentecost Gathering

APPLICATION

"Come Holy Spirit, renew the face of the earth" is a frequent refrain for the Pentecost feast and season. In this day and age, the prayer takes on an additional urgency as planetary needs are increasingly known and increasingly dire.

These prayers can be used on their own, in conjunction with a meeting, during a small faith community gathering, or within a more formal liturgy. All read the parts in bold. A sung refrain can deepen the substance of the prayer. Sadly, it often seems that written petitions can be hurried through or read perfunctorily, like a flight manifest or a laundry list. This seems a lost opportunity for people to genuinely enter into led prayer. The silence that is invited at the beginning of each prayer should not be hurried through; it is an opportunity for the assembly to really consider what is being prayed for and to bring their own energy to the petition. A resonant chime can aid the solemnity and purpose of this silence.

Leader:
Creator of the Universe,
   You hold all of life
      in Your care and keeping.
You make each of us to be
   a part of Your one tapestry
      of creation.
We bring our prayers before
   You now with great longing
      for the welfare of
         all Your people.

1) Let us pray for the whole Church, for all believing peoples.

(We pause in quiet prayer.)

Spirit of God,

Bless and inspire all people who seek to serve You in truth.

Bless the Church with gifts of every kind.

Help us to use the gifts you have given us to bind together our broken planet.

We pray together,
   God of Human Hearts:

Renew the face of the earth!

2) Let us pray for the leaders of all governments and powers.

(We pause in quiet prayer.)

The Long Arc of the Spirit: Summer Feasts

Spirit of God,

> Transform the leaders of all nations and powers, great and small.
>
> Let not our differences in language, culture, and religion impede our working together for the good of all the planet.
>
> Inspire the leaders of our own nation to overcome obstacles that keep peoples isolated and at war.

We pray together,
God of Justice:

> Renew the face of the earth!

3) Let us pray for this community of faith.

(We pause in quiet prayer.)

Spirit of God,

> Pour out Your abundant grace upon all those who are dedicated to serving You.
>
> Help us always to see the power of our calling and to cultivate the beauty of our diversity.
>
> Show us how to grow in greater unity and charity.

We pray together,
God of Wisdom:

> Renew the face of the earth!

4) Let us pray for the many people of the Earth who are struggling to simply live.

(We pause in quiet prayer.)

Spirit of God,

> Pour out Your love and consolation in the hearts of those who find life burdensome.
>
> Bless those who are homeless, those without jobs, and those who experience famine and warfare in their homelands.
>
> Give Your divine aid to those whose lives have been undone by natural and human disaster, and place within each of us the desire and the will to help those in need.

We pray together,
God of Healing:

> Renew the face of the earth!

5) Let us pray for a deeper understanding of the gift of life.

(We pause in quiet prayer.)

Spirit of God,

> You are the source of all being. Help us to cherish life more fully.
>
> Assist those who aid the healing of others.
>
> Give us the compassion, wisdom, and courage to reach out to those who experience pain and sickness in body, mind, or spirit.
>
> Let Your Spirit rest on those we remember now who are in need of Your care.

(We name aloud those who need healing.)

We pray together,
God of Creation:

> Renew the face of the earth!

6) Let us pray for those who have died.

(We pause in quiet prayer.)

Spirit of God,

> You transcend the mystery of our life here and our life beyond.
>
> Help us to trust in Your presence at all times.
>
> Grant eternal rest to those who have died, especially those from our community of families and friends, whom we remember now.

(We name aloud those who have died.)

We pray together.
   God of Eternal Life:

Renew the face of the earth!

---

7) Spirit of God, pour out Your compassion and understanding on all of us gathered here and in people everywhere.

(We pause in quiet prayer.)

> **Give us the ability to see that we are part of a larger, beautiful work.**
>
> **Grant us the grace of gratitude for all You have given us, especially the gift of all the people who help us to know love.**
>
> **Grant that we may live lives worthy of our calling in You, lives of action and contemplation and service.**
>
> **Help us to be vessels of Your presence and compassion wherever we are.**

We pray together,
   God of All Peoples:

Renew the face of the earth!

LEADER: O Great Spirit, hear these prayers and all the prayers spoken in the many languages of the earth. Hear as well those prayers uttered in the silent language of the human heart.

Let Your powerful Spirit move over all our broken lives to restore us and to bind us together in the fabric of the planet. We make our prayer together in the name of the one You have sent, Jesus,
our Brother and Lord,
 forever and ever.

AMEN.

■ ■ ■

The Long Arc of the Spirit: Summer Feasts

A Group Reflection
On the Gifts of the Holy Spirit

BACKGROUND

Seven gifts of the Holy Spirit are described in the *Catechism of the Catholic Church*, originating from an ancient consideration of virtues and ethical characteristics. This classic list includes: wisdom, understanding, counsel, knowledge, fortitude, piety, and fear of the Lord (sometimes translated as wonder or awe). But as far as gifts given to animate the body of Christ and to aid in the transformations of lives, the list can include many more descriptions and roles: peacemaker, consoler, caretaker, teacher, artist, musician, mirth-bringer, encourager, bringer of order, voicer of prayer, etc.

APPLICATION

This simple reflection can be done alone or in a group, on its own or in the context of a retreat or evening of reflection. It would be a useful exercise for parish meetings where the faithful need to stir up their own awareness of their many gifts. Perhaps it would be useful with a group of about-to-be or newly confirmed. Appropriate music can accompany any part of the service, depending on local resources.

SET UP

Have seven candles (for the gifts of the Spirit) on a central table. Paper and pens are needed for writing, and a vessel of some sort to hold papers with written gifts. Icons/artwork representing the outpouring of the Spirit might be set up. Additional candles may be used to honor the gifts of each individual. There is an option for a simple anointing with oil.

CALL TO PRAYER

Give some explanation of the Spirit as gift-bringer. What is the purpose of the gifts? How do we recognize gifts as coming from the Spirit? What do they do for the community? For the gifted person? Light seven candles (for the main gifts). Call upon the Spirit (in song or invocation).

Begin with the reading from 1 Corinthians 12. Use thoughtful silence as a way of clearing the interior stage for possibilities of a freely invited Spirit.

GREETING AND EXPLANATION OF THE SCOPE OF THE PRAYER

INVOCATION OF THE SPIRIT

(*Song, silence, or a prayed invocation.*)

A Reading:
1 Corinthians 12:4–11

(*After the reading*)
Hear how the Spirit is at work among us.

Thanks be to God.

(*A period of silent reflection.*)

A Meditation
(*Read by a reader, thoughtfully, slowly enough to digest.*)

We each have been given a gift. Perhaps, like much of the Spirit's work, it has come to us anonymously, quietly, something slipped into our lives as simple as a phone call or the greeting of a friend.

Perhaps it has arrived like fire, with force and urgency, or like the dawn, gradually unfolding and transforming everything.

We welcome the gift, we embrace it, we lay it aside, we wait to investigate its curious richness at a later time, we share it, we hoard it, we hide it away, we discount it, we undervalue it, we wait for instructions, or wonder what it may cost.

The gift comes unbidden and awaits its particular flowering in us each, in ways simple, grand, wise, loving, diligent, or generous.

It becomes as breath, light, second sight, intuition, guide, annoyance, dream.

We each shape it and give it flesh and wings.

It dies without us.

As we live, we come to know that our gift is our calling, our mission, our way of transforming ourselves and the world around us.

Our gifts are part of us. They are part of a larger group, perhaps larger than we realize.

Our gifts are hope for our shared future and worthy of true celebration.

A TIME OF REFLECTION

(With paper provided, or journals, or with collage materials, etc.)

- What can I recognize as a gift within me?
- What gifts may have been identified in me by others that I am not sure I can yet claim as mine?
- What difference do I see my gifts make in the communities of which I am part?
- What gifts do I feel are hidden in me that need to come out?
- What encouragement or guidance do I need for the growth of my gifts?
- Is there a single particular gift that I feel I have to offer?

(Write this gift on the paper provided.)

A TIME OF NAMING

(Each person [as numbers allow] takes the paper with the specific gift to the center of the space and deposits it in a vessel [treasure box, clay vessel, etc.]. The following formula is used, or a variation thereof.)

My Name is _____.

I bring the gift of _____.

(Community response)

_____, thank you. We welcome your gift.

OPTION FOR SONG

(E.g., "We Are Many Parts" [Haugen]; during the song, oil may be used to anoint the hands and forehead of each person in an act of confirmation of their gifts.)

(Each person lights a taper from the seven candles in the center of the space.)

CLOSING PRAYER

Leader: My friends,
We have gathered here
in the power of the Holy Spirit,
the One promised by Jesus
   to his disciples.

Through the inspiration
   of the Spirit,
men and women came to share
the stories of Jesus of Nazareth,
and they transformed lives.

The gifts of the Spirit
   gave birth to
communities that taught,
   healed,
loved, and served;
and they transformed a world.

We believe that the same Spirit
that moved the disciples beyond
fear and uncertainty
moves us in similar
   and mysterious ways.

And that Spirit also continues
   to give gifts
for the enlivening of the body
   of Christ,
of which we are all part.

Let us go forth into the world,

acknowledging the gifts that
 are given to each of us,
ready to encourage one another
 in the sharing of those gifts,
and eager to seek out the gifts
 of the Spirit
that are waiting in all those
 we meet.

Let us go in the Spirit of Peace,
 to be the gift of peace to the
 world through Christ.

Thanks be to God.

OPTION FOR SONG

(E.g., "Come Thou Font of Every Blessing.")

■ ■ ■

A Pentecost Table Prayer

(We begin by pouring out a cup of wine for each person. The prayer is read responsorially as directed. All read the parts in bold type.)

A: Blessed be God!

B: And blessed be the work of God's Spirit!

> **O Mysterious and Mighty
> God of the Universe,
> Your Holy Spirit
> leads us to give
>   You thanks
> through Jesus Christ.**

A: In the stunning beauty
and diversity of creation,
Your Spirit sings
in countless ways.

B: Through things seen
and unseen
by the human eye,
Your marvelous hand is at work;
Your Spirit is at play.

A: Throughout the ages
as we grow in our knowledge
    of You,
Your Holy Wisdom leads
and teaches us.

> **As humankind reaches out
> even in our seasons
>   of darkness,
> Your Spirit draws us
>   into community,
> heals us, strengthens us,
>   and renews us.
> Your Spirit brings us to life
> when we believe
>   we are dead.**

A: Touched by this Spirit,
how can we not lift our voices
with those who stand
    as witnesses
through the ages,

B: and with all the mysterious
    heavens,
praise You with full
    and joyful hearts
for Your great gift of love
    to humankind?

> **Holy and blessed are You,
> Merciful One,
> for all Your works,
> for Your unfolding Word,
> and for Your constantly
>   abiding Spirit,
> present with us now,
> present in our company
>   and at this table.
> We bless You,
>   Giver of every good gift,
> in every season.**

(We lift the bread for blessing.)

A: Blessed are You,
Holy God,
Creator of the universe,
for You give us bread to eat.
May it be our nourishment
for the journey we make
    together.

(We break the bread, pass it round the table, and eat a portion of it.)

(We lift the wine for blessing.)

B: Blessed are You,
Loving God,
Sustainer of the universe,
for You give us wine to drink.
May it be joy and grace
to refresh our souls
for the journey we make
    together.

(We take a sip of the wine together.)

> **Blessed are You,
> Holy Spirit,
> Living Breath
>   of the universe.
> In Your love,
> You give us bread and wine
> to nourish us.**

A: You give us Your consolation
to sustain us.

B. And You give us good
companions
to share the journey
    we make together
    in this world.

> **Grant us the grace
>   to be mindful,
> both in seasons of richness
> and seasons of want,
> of Your abiding presence
> and Your many gifts
> poured out within us
>   and around us,
> through Christ,
>   our Brother.**

Amen.

■ ■ ■

The Long Arc of the Spirit: Summer Feasts

The Third Sunday of June

A Blessing for Father's Day

APPLICATION

Many churches bless fathers on this holiday, though with growing sensitivity to various parts of congregations, effort is taken to be inclusive and to be careful of language that may inadvertently ostracize or offend. This prayer can be used in a congregational setting or prayed in families or on one's own.

Loving God,
Father, Protector, Teacher,
    and Friend,
we ask Your blessing this day
upon those men
who have taken
    upon themselves
the responsibility of parenting.
Guide them to be
    good role models
and loving to all their children.
Help them rely on You
to handle the challenges
    of fatherhood
in a loving way.
Help them to be both roots
    and wings
for the children they love.

And bless those who have been
    father to us
by ways other than manner
    of birth,
who have been there for us with
strength, wise counsel,
    instruction,
support, and compassion.
Bless them for their caring
    and generosity
in the ways they have helped
    us to grow.

Pour out Your healing grace
    on those
whose connections
    with their fathers
are severed by distance,
circumstance,
misunderstanding,
by anger or harsh words.
Let the grace of understanding
and Your forgiveness
gradually fill the gaps
    that are present there.

Especially tend to those
whose fathers have passed
    into Your eternal embrace
and grant that their
    appreciation and
comprehension of their fathers
    may grow
even after grief and separation.

Bless those who have lost a
    spouse to death or divorce,
who are parenting their children
    alone.
Strengthen them by Your love
    that they may become
the loving, caring persons
    they are meant to be.

Tender God,
bless all the fathers in the world
and help them to grow
    in their special role.
Grant us the grace to accept
    them as human,
with strengths and weaknesses,
who succeed and fail
    and grow through life
as we all do.

Help them to embrace their
    vocation as best they can.
Be with them in their moments
    of uncertainty and
in times that try and test them
    and their families.
Give them compassion
    for their children
and teach them the wisdom,
    humility,
and patience they need
to be a good parent, spouse,
    and partner.

We ask this
in the name of the one
    who called You
Abba
and taught us to do the same.

Amen.

■ ■ ■

Prayers of the People

For the Feast of Corpus Christi

BACKGROUND

The feast of Corpus Christi (Latin for Body of Christ), also known as Corpus Domini, is a liturgical solemnity celebrating the tradition and belief in the body and blood of Jesus Christ and his real presence in the Eucharist. It emphasizes the joy of the institution of the Eucharist, which was observed on Holy Thursday in the somber atmosphere of the nearness of Good Friday.

In the present Roman Missal, the feast is designated the solemnity of The Most Holy Body and Blood of Christ. It is also celebrated in some Anglican, Lutheran, and Old Catholic Churches that hold similar beliefs regarding the real presence.

PRAYERS OF THE PEOPLE: LITANY FROM A HUNGRY PLANET

Leader: Let us stand and pray: God of abundant giving, our ancient hungers remind us of our need for You and Your saving grace. Hear our prayers this evening for Your people, our planet, and those in need.

(Optional sung refrain: "You are All We Have" [O'Brien].)

1) The earth is hungry, Most High:

For healing from the wounds inflicted by our greed and carelessness, for restoration from storms and calamities, for a right regard by the human family for the fragile gift of our planet.

Feed the earth, O Loving God,

All: And restore Your creation to new life.

2) The Church of Christ is hungry, Holy God:

For the grace of unity and love amongst its varied and divided parts, for new clarity in its common mission, for a deeper knowledge of Your word, will, and inspiration.

Feed those who seek You, O Loving God,

With life-giving grace and guidance.

3) The nations cry out in hunger, God of All:

For peace between warring countries, for solutions to our environmental and economic disasters, for leadership that truly serves the needs of all.

Nourish Your People, O Loving God,

With wisdom, compassion, and the will to work for peace.

4) Our children cry out in hunger, Merciful God:

For freedom from want and ignorance; for an end to abuse and abandonment; for tender care and food, shelter and clothing, instruction and understanding; and for love that does not exploit.

Protect Your young ones, O Mother God,

And move us to act on their behalf with urgency and constant care.

5) And we cry out in hunger, Tender God:

For renewal and meaning in our work and lives and loves, for companionship and freedom from fear, for a deeper awareness of Your presence that heals and comforts us in seasons of pain and uncertainty.

Sustain us, O Loving God,

> **With faith that endures and with trust that You abide with us always.**

6) Loving God, we pray for those who need healing in body, mind, soul, and spirit, especially those known to us whom we name at this time.

(We name aloud those we know who are in need of healing.)

7) Eternal God, we pray for those who are near to death, for those who are in mourning, and for those dear to us who have died, especially those we name at this time.

(We name aloud those we know who are connected to the mystery of death and loss.)

8) And let us pray in thanksgiving for the many gifts of life: for love and joy and mystery, for family that connects us, friendships that nourish us and the gift of the seasons in their passage. Let us remember those who are celebrating birthdays and anniversaries among us:

(People come forward who are celebrating special moments in life.)

O God, our Source and Sustainer, we stand in need of Your grace at every moment. Draw us always to that which truly feeds and nourishes us. Make us mindful of how we are fed, and help us to live in gratitude for all that You give to us each day.

In the name of Christ, we lift our prayer.

(Optional sung refrain: "You are All We Have" [O'Brien].)

THE SIGN OF PEACE

Leader: The peace of the risen Christ be with you.

All: And also with you!

(The congregation exchanges a sign of peace.)

CLOSING PRAYER

Leader: Let us pray:

Abundant God, we thank You for gathering us here,
in our strength
    and in our weakness,
in our fullness and in our need.
We count ourselves blessed
to be fed by You with
    this heavenly food
and to be in
    one another's company,
where we know You are present.

Nourish and strengthen us
for our mission in the world.
Let Your word,
proclaimed and shared
    among us,
transform the way we think,
and feel, and act.

Grant that
in breaking the bread
and sharing the cup,
we will be made ready
to feed the world
wherever we encounter
human hungers.

Help us to know Your presence
deeply in these days
    of uncertainty,
that we may be Your presence
    to others
and bring hope and healing
through Your Spirit.
Through Christ, our brother
    and Lord,

Amen.

■ ■ ■

A Summer Service

Of Light with Bread Blessing

APPLICATION

Summertime in churches often means a decrease in attendance as parishioners travel. There are often visitors to our communities. Choirs take a needed break from Sunday service. Most churches do some battle with increased heat, and there is a general hunger for something lighter, fresher, and, perhaps, different.

This service might be well suited as an observation of the summer solstice, when the days start to become shorter. Depending on the shift of the calendar, the summer solstice occurs sometime between June 20 and June 22 in the northern hemisphere.

The following is intended as an informal service, perhaps later on the Sabbath day (near evening) as people return from picnics, outings, and bike rides. It is a service that has elements of familiar liturgical language, but it especially focuses on the blessings of light, warmth, growth, and summer vitality.

SET UP

Perhaps best advertised as a "come as you are" informal liturgy, this could take place in a park, a church garden, or someone's home. Suggestions for music are given below, but, of course, many other options exist based on the repertoire of each community and the capabilities of its musicians. The service begins with a blessing of light that can be done with candles, perhaps especially as daylight is fading. Since the format is a little out of the ordinary, worship aids of some sort are helpful. All read the parts in bold.

GATHERING

(*All rise; optional music: e.g., "When the Summer Sun Is Shining."*)

Leader: My friends, the grace of God our Creator, the peace of our Lord Jesus Christ, and the tender mercy of the Holy Spirit be with you all.

All: And also with you.

As we gather near the end of this summer day, we are mindful of the great and powerful gift of light in our lives as we enjoy the beauties of longer days.

With this in mind, let us begin with a Sabbath blessing of light. Let us pray:

(*The following may be shared by readers or read by a leader, or variations thereof.*)

Blessed are You, Holy God! When You said: "Let there be light," there was light, and it was good. When Your people fled from oppression, You led them with a pillar of fire. In Jesus Christ, Your light shines in the darkness, and the darkness cannot overcome it.

Blessed are You, God of light! Shine in our lives with the light of Christ that we might give You praise, through him who lives and reigns with You and Holy Spirit, now and forever. **AMEN.**

(A song of praise: e.g., "Evening Hymn: O Radiant Light" [Phos Hilaron].)

(During this song, candles are lit in the center, at the table, etc.)

A COMMUNAL PRAYER FOR SUMMER LIGHT

Let us pray together.

O Radiant God, in this summer season, we give You thanks for surrounding us with the gifts of light: the beauty of colors blooming all around us, the growth of crops, the length of days, the blessings of warmth, and the flow of energy we feel within us. As we draw nearer to the close of this Sabbath day, make us mindful of how much we have received through Your Providence. Grant that the light of gratitude might shine constantly within our hearts and minds, and help us to remain conscious of all that is good around us and within us, so that we may be fully alive in the brightness of Your Holy Spirit; through Jesus Christ our Lord. Amen.

LESSONS FOR THE SERVICE

(Other readings may be chosen.)

THE FIRST READING: Ezekiel 17:22–24

(After the reading:)

Hear how the Spirit is working in the Church.

Thanks be to God.

(We observe a moment of silence.)

PSALM: Psalm 92:1–4, 11–14

(Read antiphonally as instructed.)

It is a good thing to give thanks to You, Lord, and to sing praises to Your Name, O Most High;

A: To tell of your lovingkindness early in the morning and of Your faithfulness in the night season;

B: On the psaltery, and on the lyre, and to the melody of the harp.

A: For you have made me glad by Your acts, O God; and I shout for joy because of the works of Your hands.

B: The righteous shall flourish like a palm tree, and shall spread abroad like a cedar of Lebanon.

A: Those who are planted in the house of the Lord shall flourish in the courts of our God;

B: They shall still bear fruit in old age; they shall be green and succulent;

A: That they may show how upright God is, my Rock, in whom there is no fault.

It is a good thing to give thanks to You, Lord, and to sing praises to Your Name, O Most High;

(Observe a moment of silence.)

GOSPEL: Mark 4:26–34

A Reading from the holy Gospel according to Mark.

Glory to You, Lord Jesus Christ.

(After the gospel:)

Hear how the Spirit is working in the Church.
Thanks be to God.

A REFLECTION
(There is a period of silence after the reflection.)

A SUMMERTIME LITANY OF PETITION

(Prayed as directed, below.)

LEADER: Brothers and sisters, the beauty of challenges of this season still remind us that we are surrounded by need. So let us pray: Most Holy One, Your

The Long Arc of the Spirit: Summer Feasts

ancient promise is that You are a light that is near to us in every moment. We now offer our prayers to You and ask that Your Holy Spirit help us to pray with fidelity, confidence, and courage.

(Optional sung refrain: e.g., "You are All We Have" [O'Brien].)

A: Creator God, we pray for the Earth, its waters and skies, its lands and deeps, and all its varied creatures and peoples.

B: In this time of crisis and choices, may Your Spirit lead us to more carefully tend for our planet home.

A: Holy God, we pray for all believing peoples, all the faithful, their leaders, and all who minister for good.

B: In this age of transitions, change, and growth, may Your Spirit lead us to broader visions, more forgiving hearts, and more trusting wills.

(Optional sung refrain.)

A: God of Mercy, we pray for the nations of the earth, their leaders, their governors of economic powers, and all their people, especially those in pain.

B: In this time of tumult and tension, may Your Spirit lead the hearts of those entrusted with power of all kinds. Help our leaders to act with greater wisdom and with true compassion for those without power.

A: God of Light, we pray for this community of faith, all its ministers, and all its people.

B: In our worship, work, and service, may Your Spirit draw us to the truth of each of our callings. Animate the Spirit's many gifts among us for the good of those who enter this place, and for those to whom we reach beyond our doors.

(Optional sung refrain.)

A: Renewing God, we pray for Your blessings in this summer time of year.

B: In these months of beauty, growth, and fruitfulness, uphold those who grow crops for the sustenance of the human family. Give us the grace to enjoy this season and its blessings, and be with those who find its times of heat a burden.

A: Loving God, we pray for those who need healing in body, mind, soul, and spirit, especially those we name at this time.
(We name aloud those we know who are in need of healing.)

(Optional sung refrain.)

A: Eternal God, we pray for those who are near to death, for those who are in mourning, and for those dear to us who have died, especially those we name at this time.
(We name aloud those we know who are connected to the mystery of death and loss.)

A: Abiding and Trustworthy God, we pray for the situations in our lives that lead us to fear and anxiety.

B: Release us from terrors of the unknown and apprehension over things we cannot control.

(Optional sung refrain.)

LEADER: God our life, we stand in need of Your grace at every moment. Keep us fervent in our prayer and help us to be ready to act on that grace and to trust always in Your mercy and compassion. Through Christ our Lord. **AMEN.**

SHARING THE PEACE

My brothers and sisters, the

peace of the risen Christ is with you.

Let peace shine within us and around us.

(Members of the congregation exchange a sign of peace.)

THE PRESENTATION

(Bread and fruit of the vine are presented from the community to a leader [along with any other offering of the community].)

(Music at the presentation: e.g., "Prayer of Peace" [Haas].)

(Additional candles may be lit for the blessing rite.)

A SIMPLE SUMMER THANKSGIVING

(Gathered around the table, we stand [as people are able] throughout the following.)

(The Leader lifts the gifts in offering.)

We bring to You, O God, these gifts,

Which are the gifts You have given through the earth to us!

Do you know God shines within you?

God's light is within us all!

Do you have eyes?

We have eyes to see, in our heads and in our hearts. Let our eyes be open!

Do you have ears?

We have ears to hear, in our heads and in our hearts. Let our ears be open!

And do you know why you are here?

We have come in freedom to give thanks to God our Light, the Loving One who shines within us all.

It is a good thing, Most High, to give voice to our gratitude to You, O Shining One, Source of our being.

This summer season, with its beauty and power, with its shows of strength and tenderness, with its storms and gentle mornings, shows that our world is full of marvelous life.

A life that You have given in love, O Gracious God!

We are among the women and men who for countless ages have seen Your work alive in Your Creation.

A wondrous work that You have made in love, O Mighty God!

We are among those who see what You have done, who stand in awe and wonder, and who are moved by Your Holy Spirit to sing with all Your creatures our ancient song of joy:

(Sing a simple song of praise.)

We are among those who bless You, Most High God, through Jesus Christ,

Who shared our human flesh and walked among us to show us what we may yet become.

We are gathered here at this table by the summoning of the Spirit to share a meal in remembrance of the blessings that are poured out upon us, the body of Christ.

(The bread is lifted in blessing by a leader.)

We give thanks, O God, for bread that we bless—

Gathered from grain sprung from the earth: the many broken to become one.

We break it and share it, knowing how we too must be broken and shared for the world in need.

May it sustain us, O God, and give us strength.

The Long Arc of the Spirit: Summer Feasts

(The fruit of the vine is poured out and lifted in blessing by a leader.)

We give thanks, O God, for the fruit of the vine that we bless—

Crushed from the fruit sprung from the earth: the one gift poured out for the thirst of many.

We pour it and share it, knowing how we too must be poured out for the world in need.

May it delight us, O God, and revive us.

(The fruit of the vine is passed and shared by all.)

Therefore, with these good gifts, O God of all seasons and times, we bless You in this season of abundance.

May this banquet help us to know You better and to live with greater joy that call that has been given to us through Christ, our Brother.

(Optional song of thanksgiving: e.g., "The King of Love My Shepherd Is.")

PRAYER AFTER THE MEAL

Gracious God, as You have taught us to call the evening, the morning, and the noonday one day; and have made the sun to know its going down:

Dispel any darkness of our hearts and fill us anew with Your saving light. Feed us always with the food of earth as our need demands, that by Your brightness revealed in bread and cup we may know You to be the true God and eternal light, living and reigning for ever and ever. AMEN.

A CLOSING PRAYER

Let us pray together:

Blessed God, Spring of our Spirit, Summer of our souls, thank You for the gift of this gathering. Thank You for all that is gracious about this summer evening: the setting of the sun, the passing of the light, the advance of a summer night of stars.

In breaking the bread, in sharing the fruit of the vine, we are made mindful of how the Earth sustains us, despite our rough use of her.

May gathered grain and crushed grape be gifts that are simple enough and powerful enough to remind us of how we are connected to You through this marvelous gift of Earth.

By our gathering at this table, may we remember that every table can be a bridge to the sacred and a window to what is most deeply human.

May our evening prayer serve to stir up in us Your ever-enduring flame so that we may indeed be genuine lights in the world, ready to shine with Your light wherever we live, work and love.

AMEN.

BLESSING AND DISMISSAL

May God bless us all, God who Creates, Christ who Saves, and the Spirit who Sanctifies.

AMEN.

Our meal is ended. Let us go forth in the Light of the Spirit to shine with the presence of Christ wherever we live, and work, and love.

Thanks be to God.

CLOSING SONG

(E.g., "Onward To The Kingdom" [Haas].)

July 22, The Feast of Mary Magdalene

A Table Prayer

BACKGROUND

For generations miscast (by a misreading of Scripture) as the gospels' fallen woman, Mary of Magdala has been rediscovered in many ways as the "apostle to the apostles," the first to relate the stunning news of the resurrection to a group of devoted, if scared, men.

APPLICATION

For this day often lost late in the summertime lineup of feasts and holidays, a service constructed with the Magdalene in mind draws our attention to the sometimes ignored breadth of disciples who attended to Jesus. Discipleship is not just a male occupation, and the gifts of women for Christian communities have a powerful precedent in Mary. This service would be especially powerful for a women's retreat, but perhaps more useful for a mixed community.

SET UP

Several icons exist of Mary Magdalene, and such can prove to be useful for a prayer environment with table and flowers. Such an icon would be well balanced by an icon of the resurrected Christ. Music as local resources can provide is encouraged. Some suggestions are listed below. The format is assuredly out of the ordinary, so worship aids of some sort are helpful. A beautiful (painted, embroidered, etc.) processional banner of Mary would be a wonderful addition to the celebration. There is bread enough for the assembly, the fruit of the vine, and candlelight.

CALL TO PRAYER

If information is not included as part of the reflection, some history of the saint is appropriate as a preamble to the service. For meditation before we begin, we might consider those who have brought us the Good News in our lives, especially those women who played a role in making us aware that "He is risen, just as he said."

CALL TO PRAYER

(As indicated)

(Option for gathering song: e.g., "The Lord Is Risen To Life" [Mudd].)

GREETING

Leader: My sisters and brothers,
we are gathered as a community
   that has been formed
by the faithful witness of others.

Like the other apostles
   and the many disciples,
Mary Magdalene has
   a special place among those
     who observed
the works and words of Jesus
   of Nazareth.

She is counted as the first
   witness of the resurrected
     Christ,
and stands as a special icon
   of devotion and love.

Our prayer is an indication
   of the love that we are
     invited to
and a reminder that we are to
   always be an Easter people.

Let us pray together:

ALL: O Wondrous and Living God, Your Son renewed the body and mind of Mary Magdalene. His words and deeds shaped her soul and drew her into deep discipleship. May our prayerful gathering draw us closer to knowing her example of following the Rabboni of Nazareth and deepening our devotion to the One whose risen presence we celebrate in our gathering, in whose name we pray through the Spirit. **AMEN.**

THE PROCLAMATION OF SCRIPTURE

FIRST READING:
Song of Solomon 3:1–4

(After the reading:)

Hear how the Spirit speaks to the Church.

Thanks be to God.

RESPONSORIAL PSALM
(Music: some setting of Psalm 63: e.g., "I Long For You" [Balhoff, Daigle, Ducott].)

Second Reading:
2 Corinthians 5:14–18

(After the reading:)

Hear how the Spirit speaks to the Church.

Thanks be to God.

(Optional gospel hymn: e.g., "Now the Green Blade Rises.")

GOSPEL: John 20:11–18

(After the gospel:)

Hear how the Spirit speaks to the Church.

Thanks be to God.

A REFLECTION
(This may be a single person's prepared comments, or a group reflection on the reading. There is a period of quiet following.)

(Option for prayers of the people—spontaneous prayers from the community.)

PRESENTATION

(Bread and the fruit of the vine are presented along with any other gifts of the community. Music may accompany this action—e.g., "Lift Your Voice Rejoicing, Mary" [Hymn 190, Episcopal Hymnal, 1982].)

PRAYER OF BLESSING

(Leadership of this prayer may be shared among several people, or, depending on the size of the group, the voices may come from around the community. All read the parts in bold.)

Sisters and Brothers, can you believe it? Christ is with us!

It is true. Christ is risen among us indeed.

Are not your hearts burning within You?

Yes, truly, and we are lifting our hearts on high!

Can you give thanks to the One who has made us?

How can we help but give thanks to God!

1) O God of Mystery
and Endless Love,
we are gathered at this table
to praise You through
 Jesus Christ
for Your many gifts to us.

2) We come in thanksgiving:

for those who come to us as Christ in disguise,

for those who roll away the stones of fear and mistrust,

**for those who are faithful in
their witness
   to Your presence
   and healing love.**

3) We come in supplication
   and need:
for those crucified in this world
by indifference, hatred,
   and bigotry,

**for those whom
   poverty holds
captive and ignorance
   destroys,**

for all who dwell in darkness and
despair of care and kindness.

4) We come recognizing our
own needs:

**faith enough to live
as we are called,**

hope enough to stand against the
anger and cynicism
   of humankind,

**love enough
   to transform
   our lives and our world.**

5) We do not come alone:
we stand with the faithful people
You have called in every age.

**We stand with Mary
   of Magdala and
all holy women
   and men who
have given witness to You in
countless ways.**

6) We stand in the company
   of one another,
grateful for the witness
   known in this community.

**In our weakness
   and our strength,
we stand together
   in Your presence,
awaiting the daily bread
   that sustains us
and the cup that renews us.**

7) Like Mary of Magdala,
in Jesus we find
reconciliation for
   a fractured world,
hope for humankind, and a love
that transcends the barriers
   of death.

**In Your Holy Spirit,
we find the presence of Jesus
alive in us still,
   healing through
   love and forgiveness.**

8) Generous God,
we ask You to
pour out Your Holy Spirit
upon all of us gathered here,

**and we ask Your blessing
   on the bread
and the fruit of the vine
that are Your gifts
   for the sustenance of
the body of Jesus Christ.**

9) For we have come
   to this table
as generations before us
   have come.

**We are full of gratitude,
love, and remembrance.
We are hungry
   for Your presence.**

(The bread is lifted in blessing.)

10) Holy One,
we offer to You this bread,
this holy gift of gathered grain
and human labor,
this gift that is already Yours.

**Bless it for our use,
for the strengthening
   of our bodies
and the renewal
   of our hearts.**

*(The bread is broken, distributed
to all, and eaten. When the bread
is eaten, the prayer continues. The
fruit of the vine is poured out and
lifted in blessing.)*

11) Gracious One,
we have come to this table
as generations before have come.

**We are full of gratitude,
love, and remembrance.
We are thirsty
   for Your presence.**

The Long Arc of the Spirit: Summer Feasts

12) Holy One,
we offer to You this fruit
 of the vine,
this holy gift of sweet grapes
and human labor,
this gift that is already Yours.

**Bless it for our use,
for the delight
 of our tongues
and the revival of our souls.**

(The fruit of the vine is distributed to all, and all drink.)

13) Therefore with these gifts,
O Ever-living God,
we recall Your great goodness
 to us.
**With bread and fruit
 of the vine,
we remember Jesus
 of Nazareth,
the fellowship shared with
 his disciples at table,
the glory of his life and works,
the pain of his cross,
and the mystery of his rising.**

14) With Mary of Magdala,
who looked for him
 with longing,
so now do we look
for his presence at our table
 of thanksgiving.

**In the faces of all who are
 gathered here, O God,
grant us the grace to see
 the face of the Beloved,
and to regard that face
 with joy and awe.**

15) May this banquet
help us to follow the command
 of Christ
more closely: that we love
 those we meet
and share what we have.

**As his life gave testament
 to Your truth,
may our lives give witness
 to Your love
that endures forever.**

16) Together with holy Mary
 of Magdala
and all who sought to follow
your will over all the ages,

**We bless You through
 Your Christ,
in the power of
 the Holy Spirit
and in the company
 of all the blessed,
for You are our God,
 forever and ever. AMEN.**

(Optional song: e.g., "Alleluia No. 1" [Fishel].)

PRAYER AFTER THE MEAL

**ALL: O God of abundance,
 even as You touched Mary
 of Magdala with deep
 and tender love,
touch and transform
 our hearts and minds
 through this meal
 of love.**

**Inspired by her example,
 help us to move from
 this experience of You,
Our Beloved One, to places
 of proclaiming
 Your risen presence.
May we recognize You
 at work in our lives
 every day.
May we hear Your call,
 spoken uniquely to each
 of us.
May Your Spirit strengthen
 us and give us courage
 for the journey
 ahead.**

We ask this through Jesus Christ, our teacher, our guide, and our source of saving grace. AMEN.

THE FINAL BLESSING

As we prepare to go, let us pray
for God's blessing.

The God of Mercy
 has called us to accompany
the lost and the defeated
 to the threshold of healing
  and compassion.

So be it!

The God of Hope has called us
 to be faithful,
despite anything that
 disappoints or discourages.

So be it!

The God of the Impossible
 has called us
to love the world enough
 to share the gospel
  of new life,
despite the darkness of death.

So be it!

May God bless us all
 for the journey ahead,
God who has Created us,
God who has Redeemed us,
God who has Sanctified us.

So be it!

Let us go in peace
 to proclaim the risen Christ
  to a waiting world.

Thanks be to God.
(A closing song: e.g., "I Know that My Redeemer Lives.")

■ ■ ■

The Long Arc of the Spirit: Summer Feasts

A Picnic Prayer

Blessed are You, O God,
Creator of the Universe,
Lord of sun
    and scuttling clouds,
Master of breezes,
Minister of all things growing,
creeping, and
fluttering by.

Through Your goodness we have
the gifts of life this day:
beautiful weather,
nourishing food,
gracious company,
and much, much more.

Keep us always mindful of
Your presence
within us and among us.

Bless us with the graces of
awareness and gratitude of
what we have been given.

Help us to share the bounty
that has been bestowed upon us.

And grant us the picnic gift
    of being
childlike often enough
to delight in the giggle,
the tickle, the hug,
and the dizzy, delicious
roll in the good, green grass.

Amen.

■ ■ ■

Part IV
As Summer Closes

A Late Summer Blessing

Of our Animal Companions

BACKGROUND

A blessing of our animal companions is often part of a service on or around October 4, the feast of St. Francis of Assisi. Certainly, this simple service is applicable for the autumn feast of that saint, but it seems that the late summer is a good time to remember the creatures that very often have been a part of our summer experiences: hikes with dogs, cats napping in sunny summer windows, birdsong let loose on a glorious morning, or ferrets running wildly in the summer grass. Often, the summer months have given us many occasions to enjoy and appreciate this vital part of the created world. It's fitting to bless the creatures that teach us so much and give us so much joy.

APPLICATION

Any time is appropriate for this service, which can be adapted for a single person, a family, or a community. The presence of the animal companion is much dependent on all the furry, feathery, or finned necessities, but it is surely encouraged. Sometimes a photograph is needed instead for the peace of the assembly. When gathering multiple breeds and types of creatures, strict order may not necessarily be a hallmark of the service, but, even in the animal kingdom, miracles happen. Just be prepared. Very young children may choose to bring their stuffed critters for the blessing. It's a lovely teachable moment.

SET UP

This one is pretty simple: critters, their people, and treats for both. Some sort of worship aid or prayer card is helpful.

GREETING AND OPENING PRAYER

(A leader welcomes all and gives a sense of the service.)

Blessed are You, God our Maker.

And blessed are the works of Your hands!

God's Peace be with you all, human and creature alike.

And also with you.

Please join in praying our opening prayer:

Most high, omnipotent, and loving God, grant Your people the grace to learn from all of Your creation, especially from the animals with whom we live and share our homes, our joys and sorrows, and a great sense of wonder. Grant that we may, for love of You, delight in all the works of Your hands with fullness of joy. We pray in the name of Jesus through the animating power of the Holy Spirit, one God, for ever and ever. Amen.

A Gospel Reading
(Matthew 6:25–33)

Reflection

THE BLESSING OF THE ANIMALS

Leader: Our help is in the name of the Lord.

All: Who has made heaven and earth.

The Lord be with you.

And with your spirit.

Creator God, our human ties with our friends of other species are a wonderful and special gift from You. They have trust in us as we have trust in You; help us always to be worthy of their trust and to treat them with respect, compassion, and right affection. We know that we are on this earth together to show forth Your abundant love and creativity. Keep us aware of the gift they are that we may not take them for granted.

Your goodness is turned upon every living thing and Your grace flows to all Your creatures. Grant to our special animal companions long and healthy lives. Give them good relationships with us and bless them for the beauty they reveal, the awe they inspire, and the gentle joy they stir up in us.

(The goodly beasts are each blessed by the leader, one by one, or as a group.)

Grant our petitions, which we pray especially in remembrance of good St. Francis of Assisi, who honored You through all Your creatures. For You are our loving God, forever and ever.

Amen.

CLOSING PRAYER

Friends, let us pray together:

Gracious God, in the blessing of these creatures, may our eyes be further opened to see how we are each a part of Your great work brought to a fullness in Jesus Christ.

May this service draw us closer to You and to one another. Strengthen us to serve all those we meet, including Your creature world. Especially make us mindful of those creatures whose very existence is imperiled by our carelessness and shortsightedness.

Give us the grace to change our harmful habits and to honor the great diversity of your mighty work.

Thus, in the world's present darkness, may Your presence shine within us to make us strong and bright and joyful instruments of Your justice and peace.

We pray together through Christ, our Lord.

Amen.

FINAL BLESSING

May God, who calls you, bless you and keep you in peace.

Amen.

May God, who is faithful, sustain you and renew you in love.

Amen.

May God, who is always present, guide you and be with you in all you do.

Amen.

May God bless us all, human and beast alike,
God who Creates,
God who Saves,
and the God who makes all things holy.

Amen.

(Treats for beast and humans alike!)

Labor Day

A Table Prayer for the Work We Do

> *"Work is love made visible. And if you cannot work with love but only with distaste, it is better that you should leave your work and sit at the gate of the temple and take alms of those who work with joy."*
>
> Kahlil Gibran

O Gracious One, source of our
   life and our living,
we thank You now for those
   who have with love
brought forth this food
   for our nourishment
      and for our delight.

We thank You for those who do
   their daily work so often
      hidden to ourselves,
work that is so essential
   for our bodies and such
      a blessing for our souls.

We thank You for those who
   work the soil, who live
      its seasons,
who worry its storms
   and droughts, who plant
      seeds with faith,
who wait for growth with hope,
   who harvest with strong labor
and with greater joy.

We thank You for those with art
   and skill who bring meals
      into being for us,
who labor long and so often
   unnamed, those who season
      and shape
the fruit of the earth, who make
   their love palpable and good,
visible to our eyes, tasty to
   our tongues, and responsive
      to our hungers.

Loving One, Maker of all
   that is good, we thank You
   again for Earth,

Your gift of love, that sustains us
   still, despite our misuse
      of her.

Make us always mindful
   of the source of the bounty
      we enjoy.

Make us more mindful of those
   with whom we must share
the bounty entrusted to us.

And we ask that the company
   we create at this table
be likewise a work of love
   and a sign of Your love alive
      and working in us.

Finally, we thank You for
   all the work of our lives,
work that is rewarding, creative,
   helpful, and even work
      that is hard.
We deeply ask Your grace
   in the lives of those
who long for work—work with
   dignity, work that sustains
      and gives meaning.

May all the work of our hands,
   hearts, and minds bring
      Your reign more fully
         upon the Earth.

Amen.

A Blessing

As Families Part for Schooling

Students
God of tenderness
   and generosity,
shower your love on the people
who have brought me
   to this place
to learn, to grow,
   and to move forward.

Family/Loved Ones:
Holy One who gives life
   and breath
to all of us, pour out
   abundant blessings
upon these young travelers
for the days and months
   to come.

Students
You who are the source
   of our strength,
thank You for the people
   who have
sustained me and challenged me
in my journey thus far:
my family, my teachers,
   and my friends.

Family/Loved Ones:
Hold these, our beloved ones,
close to You when they feel
   alone and uncertain.
Remind them of Your faithful
   presence and
care over time and distance.
Keep them strong, wise,
   and true to themselves.

Students
Give all of us grace to allow for
our mistakes and failures,
and help us to learn from them.

Family/Loved Ones:
Grant our loved ones the desire
   for wisdom.
Inspire them to seek justice
   and truth in their studies
and in their daily living.
Give them spirits ready
   for the lessons of life ahead,
and friends who will help them
   be their best selves.

Students
We know that you are a God
   whose love
draws us together, even in times
   of silence
and across the distance
   of many miles.
Help us to trust deeply
   in the power of
Your steadfast and faithful love.

All:
O God, you are Mother and Father to us all. Help us to be open to the changes that are before us. Grant us the grace to let go of worry and fear. Let your love guide us on our way, and may your Spirit accompany us and all whom we love. May You be with all of us to defend us, within us to keep us, before us to lead us, behind us to guard us, and above us to bless us now and always.

Amen.

∴

A Meditation

As Summer Fades

O God beyond
clocks and calendars, tell me,
how
did the universe of green,
the lengthy lingering light,
the brazen blush of blooms,
slip so readily away
to these last few
    diminishing days
where—
even in the luxury
    of perfected hours,
voluptuous with apple and pear,
redolent with vines, boasting
green and purple globes,
urgent with the last riot of
rose, geranium, cosmos,
    marigold—
there is a chill,
borne upon an intrusive breeze
    that urges in another age?

Shadowed in the wings
like a character overeager
    to play its part,
I feel impatient fall
waiting out the last lines
    of September
eloquent and gloriously robed.
She speaks of fullness,
    temperance, abundance,
the bearable beauty of being
    in rarefied space.
Her tones are round
    and radiant.
All who gaze upon her
fancy that love again is possible
and age is the illusion.

And yet, I have remembered
enough years
    of this performance
to know something of how
    the drama goes.
As magicked as I am
with this pageant of plenty,
    I know
how the set must change,
the music alter,
the plot and theme
    engage shadows
that speak more weighty lines
than sometimes I can bear.

O Trustable Author
    of this beloved play,
grant me the double-masked
    capacity
to love
all that is brilliant in these final
    summer scenes,
to risk my heart,
to find it lost to senses,
unashamed and soaked
    in opulence.

Let my applause not go mute
when autumn steps forth
to speak his threadbare lines,
to pull down the weighted
    drapes,
to reveal the necessary
    structure of
the thing that is
The Play.

Grant me
sufficient grace to embrace
    each player in his part
and enough trust to know
this is a romance and no tragedy,
that spring awaits fresh
    with a practiced part,
cloaked in laughter,
ready with tender, green lines
that are always supple
    with surprise
and wise for all their newness.

■ ■ ■